DEVIL'S ADVOCATES

ALSO AVAILABLE IN THIS SERIES

Carrie Neil Mitchell

The Descent James Marriot

Let the Right One In Anne Billson

Saw Benjamin Poole

The Silence of the Lambs Barry Forshaw

Witchfinder General Ian Cooper

FORTHCOMING

Antichrist Amy Simmonds

Black Sunday Martyn Conterio

The Blair Witch Project Peter Turner

Halloween Murray Leeder

Near Dark John Berra

Nosferatu Christina Massaccesi

Psychomania I.Q. Hunter & Jamie Sherry

DEVIL'S ADVOCATES

THE THING

JEZ CONOLLY

Acknowledgements

I would very much like to thank John Atkinson at Auteur for giving me this opportunity to wax lyrical about the subject of this book. I would also like to thank the many people, in one way or another associated with *The Thing*, who kindly gave their time and shared their opinions and experiences when contacted: Anne Billson, Todd Cameron, Stuart Cohen, Lee Hardcastle, Ronnie van Hout, Michael Matessino, 'Tony' aka 'Xidioux' and Kirk Watson. Thanks also to David Bates for his read-through acumen, to Robert Chandler for his scanning prowess and to Fredrik Jansson for his screen-grabbing dexterity. Finally I would like to thank Caroline for her fine tooth comb and for putting up with the trail of torn undergarments over the last few months.

This book is dedicated to the memory of fellow Devil's Advocate James Marriott.

First publishing in 2013, reprinted 2014 by
Auteur, 24 Hartwell Crescent, Leighton Buzzard LU7 1NP
www.auteur.co.uk
Copyright © Auteur 2013

Series design: Nikki Hamlett at Cassels Design
Set by Cassels Design www.casselsdesign.co.uk
Printed and bound by CPI Group (UK) Ltd, Croydon, CR0 4YY

British Library Cataloguing-in-Publication Data
A catalogue record for this book is available from the British Library

ISBN 978-1-906733-77-3

CONTENTS

'NOW I'LL SHOW YOU WHAT I ALREADY KNOW'

THE THING – the two words that tore through the blackness of space during the opening credits of John Carpenter's 1982 film also burned their terrible shape indelibly into my mind when I first saw them. That was not on the occasion of a viewing of the film at my local cinema; you win a prize if you were one of the few to catch it during its original theatrical run in the UK. Neither was it courtesy of home video; I was 17 when the film was first released onto the video rental market, back in the days prior to the Video Recordings Act 1984 when under-18s could get to see all manner of horrors entirely at the discretion of their local video shop owner.

No, I first witnessed those eight letters incinerating their way across the screen during a BBC TV news report concerning the dangers to society of so-called 'video nasties' and the moral panic surrounding the availability of supposedly mind-melting visual material. Among others mentioned in the report were those hardy perennial shockers *I Spit on Your Grave* (Meir Zarchi, 1978), *The Driller Killer* (Abel Ferrara, 1979) and *The Evil Dead* (Sam Raimi, 1981), but it was a shot of the *Thing* titles, filmed appearing on a television screen in an ordinary domestic British lounge with two impressionable adolescent boys watching it, that caught my eye and piqued my interest. There's a very similar image midway through Carpenter's 1978 hit *Halloween*; babysitter Laurie Strode (Jamie Lee Curtis) allows her young charge Tommy (Brian Andrews) to stay up and watch the late night movie, which happens to be the 1951 Howard Hawks-produced/Christian Nyby-directed *The Thing from Another World*. There they are, those two words flickering in black and white, just as they would be at the beginning of Carpenter's remake. There's a very similar screen-watching moment in the Carpenter *Thing* itself; we see the men of the American Antarctic research station US Outpost 31[1] viewing the video footage salvaged from the wrecked Norwegian base as they witness the moment caught on camera when the fated Scandinavian team encircle the saucer that they have discovered in the ice, a near exact match for the saucer discovery scene in Hawks' picture.

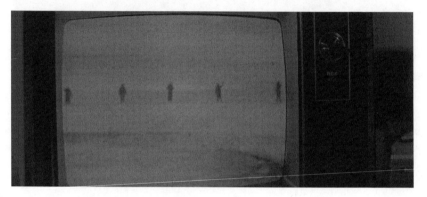

The Norwegian team encircle the saucer.

But terrifying as it was, *The Thing* never actually troubled the Director of Public Prosecutions' hit list, that notorious roll call of supposed movie atrocities that first appeared in June 1983 of which 39 were subsequently prosecuted under the Obscene Publications Act and effectively banned. The nearest *The Thing* got to being banned under the Act was in Hampshire where police seized copies after a magistrate, having cleared a video dealer on eight counts relating to films on the banned list, proceeded to order that copies of Carpenter's film be destroyed. Unless you happened to be living in Finland at the time where the film was initially banned it wasn't too difficult a title to find and watch once it had received its release on tape.

However it didn't entirely escape the tabloids' moralistic searchlights in the early 1980s. Somewhat arbitrarily within the space of a few months it featured in reports concerning two serial rapists; before being convicted of the rape of two women and sentenced to two life terms Christopher Meah claimed that *The Thing* had had a major influence on his actions. Perhaps less spuriously Meah's defence also claimed that his behaviour had been caused as a result of a car crash, which led later to a notoriously controversial compensation payout to the convicted party, an outcome that tends to overshadow his *Thing* obsession in subsequent reporting of the case. Shortly after the Meah trial made the news a reference to *The Thing* cropped up again, this time in the case of Malcolm 'The Fox' Fairley, a multiple rapist who displayed an indiscriminacy towards his victims – male, female, even a family pet dog – of which the Thing itself would have been proud. Seized with the mania of the day that sought to pin every moral violation on the existence of horror films on tape, the press claimed that Fairley was a 'video nasty fan', a conclusion which appears to be based largely on the fact that he stole two videotapes from the premises of one of his attacks, one of which was *The Thing*. For the record, the other tape was *National Lampoon's Animal House* (John Landis, 1978), which might just explain his penchant for canines.

Thinking back to that BBC News report, I can only assume that the film crew responsible for the footage picked *The Thing* for the two boys to watch because they considered it to be especially illustrative of the graphic horror film of the times and, ironically, was a tape they could readily get their hands on. I've often imagined since that the two boys were the journalist's nephews who were coerced into watching those opening credits with the promise of a bag of sweets and a chance for one of them to be seen on television sporting their new electric blue satin windcheater, the one with the eagle embroidered on the back.

I wanted to experience that frisson of fear that these two adolescents had been allowed access to. They were younger than me for starters, which annoyed me greatly, and the tenor of the report suggested that we might be a matter of weeks away from some kind of blanket ban on films of this nature. I determined to get my feet wet while I still had the chance, and so as a direct result of seeing that damning news report warning me of the perils of the modern horror movie, I rented a copy of *The Thing* while I still could. The video shop owner across the road from where I lived was a fat chain-smoker who had a whole wall of horror; *Cannibal* this, *Holocaust* that, *Zombie* the other, shelf after shelf of large format videotape cases, all bearing the stock lurid airbrushed artwork synonymous with the glut of cheap horror flicks being pushed out in the early 1980s.

He displayed no qualms about lending me his copy of *The Thing*, nor did he ask me for any proof of age. Why would he? The law at that point didn't require him to.

So I took the tape home and watched it in all its poorly transferred, pan and scan glory, fully expecting to be morally disembowelled by the experience. Somehow I survived. I'd be lying if I told you that it didn't give me one or two nightmares. If I'm honest it still does, which helps to explain why over the years I have been repeatedly drawn back to it. I'm fairly sure that horror cinema audiences, and writers for that matter, are compelled to return to their favourites in an attempt to understand why the films scared them in the first place. Most of my own recent experiences of re-watching the horror films that I saw when I was younger have led to disappointment – apologies to any Freddy Krueger fans reading this but these days I find very little that unsettles me in the original version of *A Nightmare on Elm Street* (Wes Craven, 1984) and its numerous sequels – so there has to be something about *The Thing* that compels me to revisit it.

In the years since its release *The Thing* has come to represent the ultimate 'clunker to cult to classic' movie journey. Its initially poor critical and commercial reception is now the stuff of legend; few films can claim to have bounced back quite so spectacularly in the long run from quite such a press drubbing and audience no-show. Anne Billson's excellent 1997 BFI Modern Classics book on the film, until now still the only dedicated, substantive, widely available monograph on the subject, was published fifteen years after the release of John Carpenter's film. In a recent interview for the film's fantastically exhaustive fan website Outpost#31, Billson tried to explain why *The Thing* generated such a dismissively scornful reaction from film journalists:

> Critics seem to pride themselves in remaining unaffected by the films they're watching, and they tend to watch horror films at ten thirty in the morning, surrounded by other critics, which isn't the ideal situation in which to see a horror movie – I bet if they were obliged to watch horror movies after midnight, on their own, their opinions would change. The only reaction they permit themselves is a sort of wry intellectual amusement, and if they have been traumatised they're never going to admit it. Admitting that you have been disturbed by a horror film is tantamount to admitting that the film works, and that you yourself are vulnerable to the same fears as everyone else, and since part of horror's power is primal rather than intellectual, it's

preferable to remain detached rather than start digging around in your own psyche, maybe uncovering things about yourself you'd prefer not to have to confront. Flippant dismissal, with or without sneering, enables critics to demonstrate in public not only that the film hasn't got to them, but that they're regular human beings and NOT AT ALL sick or twisted or frightened. (Billson/Outpost#31, 2012)

Through her book Billson can take a great deal of credit for prompting the reappraisal of the film that began in the late 1990s; in the years since that book's publication *The Thing* has, as it were, emerged fully formed from the deep freeze of its initial reception to become one of the most highly regarded productions from the 'Body Horror' cycle of films during the 1980s and has gone on to inform the wider body of modern horror cinema.

If there is a cycle to these things then now is the time to revisit Carpenter's film, as much has happened since 1997 to warrant its further examination. *The Thing* was first released on DVD on 9 September 1998, a disc that included a lengthy 'making of' documentary, *The Thing: Terror Takes Shape*, which served to populate fans' knowledge base on the production. This DVD release of the film, coupled with the embryonic stages of internet fan culture – the Outpost#31 website went online in October 2001 – has led to a wholesale and detailed reappraisal of the film that has secured its place in the pantheon of modern cinematic horror.

A fair percentage of the earliest serious academic analyses of the film tended to focus on how much its themes of contagion, paranoid terror and blood tests in an all-male environment were analogous to the rapidly growing concerns over the AIDS virus around the time of its release. While there is much merit in this thesis it's a point that has already been fairly well explored and, I would argue, is a rather pat, simplistic critique, one based on the presumed intentions of the film's makers that overlooks the possibility of coincidence, all of which serves to overshadow what else is going on in the film. For instance there are some interesting gender/sexuality-related issues other than AIDS that are there to be explored, which you'll find in this analysis.

Unlike Anne Billson's BFI book – which remains an authoritative response to the film and one I would strongly recommend reading – this volume in the *Devil's Advocates* series will avoid a linear 'walk through' the film's plot as its umbrella analytical device and instead focus on a mix of themes that demand further exploration. It will naturally place the Carpenter film at the centre of the discussion and in so doing it will treat the film as a pivotal device for looking back to its antecedents, principally the John W. Campbell Jr. 1938 novella *Who Goes There?* and the 1951 Hawks/Nyby film, and forward to the changing nature of its reception and the work that it has influenced, including the 2011 prequel. In some respects I will use the Carpenter film in much the same way that the Thing uses human beings; I'll approach it possessing a collective race-memory of what has gone before, I'll inhabit it and draw upon it to make sense of the world around it and I'll project outwards from it to explore the territory of its reception.

Initially the discussion will encompass the significance of *The Thing*'s subversive antipodal environment, the white space of Antarctica as the film's canvas and Carpenter's emphasis on emergence from dark to light, interior to exterior. *The Thing* is a film pulled inside out set in a place on Earth where the accepted laws of physics are subject to magnetic polar anomaly, and we will see how this impinges on the nature of the film.

An examination of the monstrous forms that the Thing has assumed in its various screen outings will help to chart the journey that the concept has taken from Campbell Jr.'s original cell-copying creature in *Who Goes There?* through the Hawks/Nyby 'carrot' in the 1951 film and on to Carpenter's assimilation model and beyond.

Regarded by many as the apotheosis of his work, *The Thing* provides a good opportunity to look at some of the ways Carpenter used film-making technique to ramp up the pervading sense of paranoid fear that germinates within his characters, plays out in the film's situations and extends out into its audience. His ability to combine actor performances and restricted sets with camera positioning and movement, lighting and cutting within the wide screen aspect ratio was perhaps never put to better use than on *The Thing*.

The one aspect of the film that is most frequently raised and discussed is its special effects, and no book about *The Thing* should be without a section that sheds some light on the work of the Special Make-up Effects Unit headed by Rob Bottin. For many, the film and its visual effects were at the eye of the storm that was 1980s Body Horror, everything else revolved around it. The very special effect of Bottin's extraordinary handiwork is a major reason why new generations of viewers have continued to seek the film out. How people react to what they see when watching *The Thing* is one of my own abiding fascinations; back in those VHS days I took great pleasure in showing the film to numerous friends and family members – after that first vaguely furtive occasion I must have rented the tape four or five times in quite quick succession – and I became very interested in the way different people reacted to the numerous 'money shots'. I remain interested in the reaction it generates, especially when that reaction is laughter; maybe not what the makers of a film so seemingly serious intended but we'll look at why some viewers respond in this way.

It's notable that the film's reappraisal has coincided with the rise of CGI as the prevailing and dominant method of realising movie monsters, a technique, one might expect, that would effectively render the visuals of *The Thing* obsolete in the minds of many audiences. Conversely the film has become something of a touchstone for a growing number of followers either nostalgic for the type of visceral pre-computer generated on-set practical effects that it boasts or younger generations suffering from 'pixel fatigue'.

A major part of the discussion will concentrate on *The Thing*'s stages of revival, through VHS/Laserdisc, DVD/Blu-ray and the Web, and the odyssey it has undertaken. In *Time Out*'s 2012 list of the 100 best horror films *The Thing* reached No.6, an extraordinary indicator of the film's latter day reappreciation. Now that the film is widely acknowledged as a landmark production in the horror genre it is a timely moment to consider the changing nature of its reception, its influence on more recent productions and media and how these reflect back upon the Carpenter film. Rounding off the discussion there will be an appreciation of *The Thing*'s notoriously downbeat ending and why, despite the number of apparent loose ends, the denouement amid the burning wreckage of Outpost 31 is not quite as ambiguous as it seems. But before all of that...

'I KNOW HOW THIS ONE ENDS'

Just in case you've decided to buy and read this book and happen to have spent at least the last 100,000 years encased in a block of ice it might prove useful at this early juncture to offer a brief outline of the film's plot before we proceed. So, spoilers ahoy – but think of it as a necessary briefing in advance of the main thematic discussion. Even if you know the film inside out it won't hurt to go over the basics in order to refresh your memory. This is also a handy opportunity to provide a 'who's who', so to speak, of the cast members of the film and establish the names of the characters that Carpenter used. When looking across *The Thing*'s various literary and on-screen manifestations it can get a little confusing; names were changed or dropped in the films, several characters were either entirely new confections or more than one character from the novella distilled into a single character. There are even name differences between characters in Carpenter's film, Bill Lancaster's draft script for the film and Alan Dean Foster's otherwise fairly verbatim 1983 tie-in novelisation published by Bantam. So this sets down a record of reference for the film that forms the centrepiece of this study.

Seeing as we're talking names, let me instil a little disambiguation to help differentiate between the titles of the various *Thing* film versions. Carpenter's film is all about the loss of identity, so in the spirit of R. J. MacReady and his efforts to determine who's human and who's Thing, I can report the results of a little blood test that I devised to help you be sure which *Thing* is being discussed at any given point in the book. Any references to *The Thing from Another World* are addressing the 1951 film. It doesn't help us that between 1951 and 1982 that film was often referred to simply as *The Thing*, so on occasions, for clarity and brevity, you will also find it cited as 'the Hawks/Nyby film'.[2] From here on instances of the italicised title *The Thing* relate solely to the 1982 film directed by John Carpenter, which will also be frequently called 'the Carpenter film'. You'll know when the discussion turns to the 2011 prequel directed by Matthijs van Heijningen Jr., which also bears the title *The Thing*, because it will be referred to either as 'the *Thing* prequel', 'the van Heijningen Jr. film' or another logical combination of descriptors.

Additionally this is as an early chance to set out a few descriptive conventions and shorthand terminology for some of the key concepts and characters involved in the analysis in order to avoid lengthy repetition as the book proceeds. So for example you'll know whenever you come across a phrase like 'Kennel-Thing' later on that it's a reference to the agglomeration of sled dogs that the men of Outpost 31 find in mid-assimilation around 29 minutes into the Carpenter film. The terms used are almost exclusively drawn from the common *lingua franca* of *Thing* internet fan culture, which is not to say that this book is merely an extension of the admittedly valuable taxanomic approach to recording the minutiae of the film that the online fan community provides. It's simply an acknowledgement of the canonical language that has developed and an honest and conscious avoidance of wheel reinvention. So here goes.

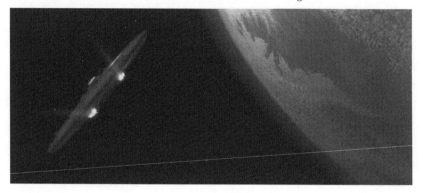

Antarctica from space, 100,000 years ago, at least.

Black screen, white upper case opening titles text rendered in the Albertus MT font, synthesised F sharp bass drone. Yes, it's a John Carpenter film! Out of the blackness emerge stars, fixed pinpricks of white that prefigure the snow storm of the film's final third. A flying saucer hurtles past; we only get a brief glimpse but it possesses characteristics of the stock intergalactic vessel seen in everything from *The Day the Earth Stood Still* (Robert Wise, 1951) onwards during the 1950s, mixed with a dash of the incandescent tilting flight path of the UFOs that populate *Close Encounters of the Third Kind* (Steven Spielberg, 1977) so right away there's a sense of something old, something new. The ship plummets towards Earth, glowing briefly as it enters the planet's atmosphere, at which point it disappears from view. What we don't know at this point, and won't know until some way in, is that we are witnessing an event that took place a long time ago. That might just be the peninsula of Palmer Land, the Weddell Sea and the Ronne Ice Shelf we can see, an inverted view compared to our more common cartographic representations of the South Polar continent but just about recognisable. Cue the terrifying blue-white film title incremation and the fade to black that announces the beginning of the story.

It's Antarctica, the winter of 1982, and seemingly open season on the hunting of dogs with rifles, at least if you're Norwegian. Enter canine (specifically an Alaskan Malamute dog actor by the name of Jed) screen right, pursued by a helicopter with 'Norge' written on the side. The dog makes a beeline for Outpost 31 where, hearing shots, several of the twelve men stationed there come out to meet him. The Norwegian chopper lands nearby and its two occupants continue their attempts to kill the poor mutt. A mis-thrown thermite grenade accounts for one of them and the helicopter, while the other pursuer shouts in Norwegian and fires off rounds in the general direction of his quarry. If only at this early point in the film just one of the guys at Outpost 31 had known even a smattering of Norwegian, perhaps all that was to come might have been avoided. 'Get the hell outta there. That's not a dog, it's some sort of thing! It's imitating a dog, it isn't real! GET AWAY YOU IDIOTS!' is how the rifleman's words actually translate. He might as well have been reading a page from the Oslo telephone directory for all the good it did. Of course we the audience are no better off in that there are no subtitles provided. Obviously there aren't; there'd be no surprises for us later if we knew what had been said, but this does perhaps explain why Norwegian-speaking viewers tend to receive the film's subsequent horrors with a look of resigned expectation. (One posted this remark beneath a YouTube clip of this sequence: 'I speak Norwegian and understand what he says. Also, it kind of spoiled the movie for me.')

One of the Americans, the meteorologist Bennings (Peter Maloney), receives a graze to his leg from one of the passing bullets before the remaining Scandinavian is fatally dispatched by Garry (Donald Moffat) the station manager with his trusty Colt Trooper revolver. Jed the Alaskan Malamute makes friends with dog handler Clark (Richard Masur). Against his better judgment, reclusive whisky-swigging Vietnam veteran and the outpost's no.1 helicopter pilot R.J. MacReady (Kurt Russell) is persuaded by the camp's physician Dr. Copper (Richard Dysart) to fly to the Norwegian base in order to investigate.

MacReady and the doctor find signs of violence and destruction, including the frozen corpse of a man who appears to have slit his own wrists and throat. There's also a huge block of ice, hollowed out as though something has emerged from it. Outside the main building lies the charred remains of, well, it's rather hard to say exactly. Let's call it the Split-Face Thing. With the weather closing in the two men decide to return to Outpost 31, taking with them these weird remains wrapped in a tarpaulin together with a portable video unit they find at the scene.

Meanwhile back at the American base Jed has been left to pad around the corridors and wander into the men's private quarters. There's definitely something not quite right with this dog. MacReady and Copper arrive back and unveil the twisted mass of tissue that they salvaged from the Norwegian base. Senior biologist Blair (Wilfred Brimley) conducts an autopsy and despite the abominable contortions of the 'corpse' discovers what appear to be a normal set of internal organs.

Meanwhile Clark comes under pressure to secure the roaming canine newcomer down in the kennel with the other sled dogs. This is the moment when we get our first view of the Thing in action; locked in with the resident hounds the interloper splits and ruptures horrifically, sprouting tentacles and arachnid appendages and squirting the other dogs with unearthly bile. The ensuing howls alert the men who arrive to find the Kennel-Thing at some midway stage of de/recomposition. Having absorbed most of the dogs, the seething mass of tissue is torched by chief mechanic Childs (Keith David) with one of the camp flamethrowers before it can attack the assembled humans, but not before part of the creature has escaped through the kennel roof. Blair is required to perform an examination of the extinguished monstrosity and theorises that what they are faced with is an organism capable of imitating other life forms. Wishing to find out more the men view the salvaged Norwegian video and observe the attempted destruction of what appears to be a gigantic extraterrestrial vehicle that has crashed and been buried in the ice. The next day MacReady, geologist Norris (Charles Hallahan) and assistant mechanic Palmer (David Clennon) fly out to the crash site. They find the damaged remains of the saucer and nearby a hole in the ice which corresponds with the hollowed out block that MacReady and Copper found at the Norwegian base.

Ratings for the Norwegian video show swell to seven.

Back at Outpost 31 MacReady does his best to explain to the others what they found at the crash site. Childs dismisses it as 'voodoo bullshit' while resident stoned conspiracy theorist Palmer insists 'Chariots of the Gods man, they practically own South America. I mean, they taught the Incas everything they know'. MacReady continues to hypothesise but is interrupted by the base's cook Nauls (T.K. Carter) who has found somebody's ripped underwear left in the kitchen trash can (we'll be seeing more shredded garments as the story progresses). Blair retires to his lab where he calculates the probability of infection rate among the men (75 per cent) and the time it would take for all of humankind to become entirely assimilated by the Thing organism should it be allowed to reach civilised areas (127,000 hours). While Blair is absorbing these frightening statistics the organism lying semi-dormant in the Split-Face Thing from the Norwegian base springs back to life and tries to assimilate Bennings. The men reach it before it has time to finish and quickly burn it. Amid this drama Blair goes missing until MacReady spots him running away from the camp helicopter, axe in hand. He has smashed the dashboard, presumably in order to stop any Thing-assimilated men escaping and making it to the mainland. Shots ring out from inside the camp. MacReady hurries back to find Blair holed up in the radio room where he has overpowered radio operator Windows (Thomas G. Waites) and is taking an axe to the communications equipment. The men manage to overcome and sedate Blair and lock him in the tool shed. As MacReady is about to leave Blair the old biologist warns his younger colleague to keep an eye on Clark, compounding MacReady's existing suspicions about the dog handler.

Copper suggests a blood test to determine if any more of the men are infected but before this can happen the camp's supply of transfusion blood is found tampered with. Accusations and arguments ensue, Windows panics and an armed stand-off takes place resulting in the now-under-suspicion Garry relinquishing his gun, and with it his authority. MacReady takes charge and asks Blair's lab assistant Fuchs (Joel Polis) to come up with another test. In conversation with MacReady, Fuchs suggests that even the smallest particle of Thing can take over an entire organism. Before he has a chance to devise a new test Fuchs pursues an unidentifiable figure out into the snow where he happens upon another pair of shredded undergarments, this time bearing MacReady's name tag. Subsequently some of the men find the incinerated remains of Fuchs who, they theorise, took his own life in despair before the Thing could get to him. More of MacReady's ripped garments emerge; Nauls, having cut MacReady loose from the guide rope that links the camp buildings, shows the others some shreds of fabric with the pilot's name on that he extricated from the furnace by MacReady's shack. Locked out in the cold and now suspected by all, MacReady gains entrance back inside the main building through the supply room where he is found holding some explosives and threatening to blow up the entire camp. Some of the men try, and fail, to disarm him, and in the process Norris collapses with a suspected heart attack. Copper administers defibrillation which triggers the Thing that is now Norris to emerge violently, chewing off Copper's arms in the process. Cue the detached Norris-Thing head, sprouting legs and attempting to scuttle off, prompting Palmer's now-famously understated reaction, 'you gotta be fucking kidding'.

MacReady decides to rig a rudimentary blood test of his own devising, but first has to repel an attack from Clark (the red herring, human after all), with fatal consequences for the dog handler. Samples of the remaining men's blood are taken and a hot needle is inserted into each to check for a reaction. Despite contrary suspicions it is Palmer's blood that leaps from the dish, prompting the Palmer-Thing to erupt out into the open and attack Windows before being destroyed. So who's left and who's human? The blood test confirms that MacReady, Nauls, Childs and Garry are all still who they say they are. But what about Blair, up in the tool shed? When they go to administer the test the men fail to find the biologist, but discover that he, or rather the Thing imitation of him, has been busy using parts from the wrecked helicopter to build a mini escape saucer. It dawns on MacReady that in order to stop the Thing making it off the base the remaining humans, himself included, probably shouldn't survive. During an attempt to destroy the camp and flush out the remaining Thing organism both Garry and (off camera) Nauls are absorbed by the Blair-Thing. Childs goes temporarily AWOL. MacReady has a final 'fuck you too!' meeting with the Blair-Thing before the camp lights up like a Christmas tree, leaving MacReady sitting by the flames to keep warm with his trusty bottle of J&B whisky for companionship. Childs reappears and the two men exchange concerns that one or either of them may be a Thing. We never do get to find out...

'FIRST GODDAMN WEEK OF WINTER'

'That's not a dog, it's some sort of thing!'

Snow: in its fresh state just about the whitest natural substance on Earth, and the cold, blank canvas upon which John Carpenter painted his lurid depiction of alien life in *The Thing*. Principal location filming in Antarctica was not an economic or logistical option, but all the same the challenges of shooting around the town of Stewart in north western British Columbia were not inconsiderable. Those glacier glasses worn by Kurt Russell weren't just a stylistic detail; snow blindness, or photokeratitis to give it its proper medical name, was a serious risk to the film's crew during the exterior shoot in British Columbia. Carpenter himself was later diagnosed with facial skin cancer as a direct result of exposure to the sun's rays reflecting off the snow.

Looking at a vast expanse of white for extended periods of time can have an interesting effect on the eyes; we perceive colour with sensory cells called cone cells which are found at the back of the eye in a tiny area called the fovea. These cone cells respond to red, green or blue occurring in the light that enters the eye. Working together in subtle combination the cone cells allow us to detect the shades and nuances of the colour spectrum, and when fully combined they detect white. However when they are exposed to a single colour for a relatively long time cone cell fatigue can kick in. So when you are in front of a snow-set scene in a film which continues for, say, at least ten seconds before cutting to a darker interior your white-drenched cone cells will have grown tired and the sudden darkness will seem extra dark.

There's also the phenomenon of afterimage; you've probably experienced one of those optical illusions where you're invited to fix your eyes exclusively on the spot on the nose of a *negative* image of somebody's face then look away at a white surface where you'll see suspended a ghostly *positive* image of Che Guevara, Jesus Christ or some such. So in a film a dark figure seen moving through a snowy waste can appear briefly as a blurry apparition for a few brief moments when a cut to darkness occurs. (We could go on to discuss Haidinger's Brush, the Purkinje tree and other entoptic phenomena but I'll leave you to google those. We'll come on to polarisation in a while.)

Think of some of the great snow scenes in films: the lone prospector finding his way through a blizzard to Black Larsen's cabin in *The Gold Rush* (Charles Chaplin, 1925); the young boy and his beloved Rosebud playing in the snow outside Mrs. Kane's boarding house in *Citizen Kane* (Orson Welles, 1941); the troika ride across the Russian Steppes towards the ice palace in *Doctor Zhivago* (David Lean, 1965). In each case the eye is allowed to absorb the brightness of the snow through prolonged exposure so that when the shot pans or cuts to a contrastingly darker interior there is a heightened visual impact and an emphasised sense of internalisation. And also isolation. The confined spaces of Outpost 31 are lit in stark directed spots; angle-poise desk lamps, surgical lights, strings of ceiling-suspended sixty watt bulbs in the narrow corridors, with only an incongruously decorative shade above the table tennis table and a collection of piss-yellow table lamps around the perimeter of the rec room providing anything resembling visual warmth. Away from the bright pools provided by the light sources shadows proliferate, lending the base a near-monochromatic bleakness. In fact over and above the red and yellow-green splatter associated with Thing transformations it's not actually that much more colourful than *The Thing from Another World* which was shot in black and white.

The frequent contemporary comparator (or progenitor, depending on your point of view) to Carpenter's *The Thing* is Ridley Scott's *Alien* (1979). However, a look at the post-credits opening few minutes of both films offers an early illustration of *The Thing*'s inside out, upside down world. In *Alien* we see the mining freighter Nostromo gliding through the blackness of space and are introduced to its interior and inhabitants through the flickering ignition of the ship's fluorescent tube lighting, an illumination that renders the white hypersleep chambers and living quarters largely shadowless. Later on of course the lights go out and the Nostromo will transform into the Old Dark House of cinema convention; but that initial black exterior/white interior switch contrasts with *The Thing*'s opposing shift from the blinding brightness of Antarctica to the spot-lit darkness inside Outpost 31.[3]

Situating the story of *The Thing* in the harsh white wilderness of the south polar region directly corresponds with the Antarctic setting of the novella upon which the film was based, which contrasts with the Hawks/Nyby McCarthy-era film that switched the action to the North Pole so as to equate the alien threat with the fears over Russian intentions at the time. First published in the August 1938 edition of *Astounding Science-Fiction* magazine, *Who Goes There?* was written by New Jersey-born John W. Campbell Jr. under the pen name Don A. Stuart. It's interesting to note that Campbell Jr.'s mother Dorothy had an identical twin sister and he was frequently unable to tell them apart, a childhood experience that may very well have informed the theme of uncertain identity in his novella. Written at the age of 28, *Who Goes There?* is a pivotal work; regarded as Campbell Jr.'s last significant piece of published fiction, it arrived at the very beginning of what has come to be known as the 'Golden Age' of science fiction, recognised as the period between 1938 and 1946, and in its own small way is the culmination of certain strands of American social and literary history relating to the South Pole that developed in the early decades of the twentieth century.

The Heroic Age of Antarctic Exploration, covering the end of the nineteenth century up to the early 1920s, is most popularly characterised by the Scott and Amundsen expeditions' race to the South Pole at the end of 1911 and Sir Ernest Shackleton's various sorties into the continent between 1901 and 1922. Aside from the United States Exploring Expedition of 1838–1842 led by Charles Wilkes, American involvement in Antarctic exploration came late to the party. It wasn't until the exploits of Richard Evelyn Byrd, whose aeroplane flight over the South Pole during his expedition of 1928–1930 awakened frontier fantasies, that the potential of Antarctica as an American concern was planted in the national psyche, leading ultimately to the US scientific presence that is found there today. Byrd's airborne endeavours secured his place in the history books and also inspired the storytellers of the day. Indeed both Byrd and another notable 1930s American Antarctic explorer Lincoln Ellsworth are referred to in passing in *Who Goes There?*

Master of the weird fiction subgenre H. P. Lovecraft had a lifelong interest in Antarctic exploration and followed Byrd's expedition closely. His novella *At the Mountains of Madness*, written in 1931 and serialised for publication in the February, March and April 1936 issues of *Astounding Stories* (as *Astounding Science-Fiction* was known at that point) drew on this abiding fascination, and was also heavily informed by Lovecraft's own quite serious hypersensitivity to cold (read his 1928 short story *Cool Air* for further evidence of this). *At the Mountains of Madness* tells of a geological expedition's discovery of ancient life forms in Antarctica and involves disappearing dogs, dissections and creatures called Shoggoths. Lovecraft described an encounter with a Shoggoth thus:

> It was a terrible, indescribable thing vaster than any subway train—a shapeless congeries of protoplasmic bubbles, faintly self-luminous, and with myriads of temporary eyes forming and un-forming as pustules of greenish light all over the tunnel-filling front that bore down upon us. (Lovecraft, April 1936: 160)

With its depiction of the waking astronaut builders of a lost civilisation that predate humankind and the interpretation of hieroglyphic murals discovered on the walls of a hidden city, *At the Mountains of Madness* bears even greater comparison with Ridley Scott's underwhelming *Alien* sort-of prequel *Prometheus* (2012), a much-touted release of recent times which was arguably responsible for the shelving of a James Cameron/ Guillermo del Toro/Tom Cruise film adaptation of the Lovecraft story that has been mooted for several years. Back in the mid-1930s *At the Mountains of Madness* had a clear influence on the young John W. Campbell Jr. and fed significantly into the themes of *Who Goes There?* In the days of Lovecraft and Campbell Jr. Antarctica remained largely unexplored despite the flurry of expeditions in the early decades of the twentieth century, allowing the writers plenty of licence to exercise their imaginations with little risk of immediate factual contradiction.

Discoveries elsewhere in the world at that time were catching up with fiction; 1938 was also the year of the Coelacanth, a prehistoric lungfish long thought extinct that turned up alive and swimming off the coast of South Africa, a wonder of the natural world which bears remarkable similarity to the idea of revivification found in all things *Thing*. The exhumation of possibly the most intact frozen mammoth remains in Siberia, now known as the Beresovka Mammoth, occurred in 1900 and a number of similar finds followed. The creature disinterred from the ice in *Who Goes There?* is initially thought by the men to be as dead as one of these giants of prehistory. Another developing branch of science in the first half of the twentieth century was paleomagnetism, the study of the patterns left by the Earth's magnetic fields in sedimentary rock or solidified volcanic larva. The American base in *Who Goes There?* is called Big Magnet and is located directly over the south magnetic pole of the Earth. The alien find that McReady (as opposed to *Mac*Ready, as spelled in the Carpenter film) unveils to his colleagues was found at the source of a magnetic anomaly situated around eighty miles south west of the base. Although the exact nature of the scientific research being undertaken at Big Magnet isn't expressly specified there's mention of the 'Secondary Magnetic Expedition' and we learn that among its team of 37 men the base is populated by several physicists, a biologist, a cosmic ray specialist and a meteorologist. McReady is the latter, and like MacReady in Carpenter's *The Thing* he emerges as the voice of authority and certainty when the crisis deepens.

In *Who Goes There?* he is repeatedly characterised as possessing bronze-like qualities; he is a 'looming bronze statue' with a 'great red-bronze beard', 'bronzed hands' and a 'lean, bronzed face'. Bronze as you probably know is not a magnetic material, unlike nickel, cobalt, steel and iron. A number of the other men at Big Magnet are lent magnetic metal attributes, often in direct comparative opposition to McReady; Norris is 'all steel', Connant is an 'ironman', Benning possesses 'wiry strength' and Kinner has a 'brass throat and cast-iron larynx'. The implication is that all but McReady the man of bronze could be susceptible to the influence of the magnetic anomaly that is the Thing. There is also an explicit suggestion in the novella, not clearly picked up in the Carpenter film, that the Thing possesses telepathic capabilities, allowing it to invade the minds of the men – Blair describes it as 'dream-infectious' – and begin the process of assimilation at a psychological level before it moves on to the corporeal copy-and-paste. While McReady is not immune to this he demonstrates a greater resistance than the others which again separates him and presents the greater group as a controlled cluster under the influence of the Thing.

Although there's nothing especially bronzed about Kurt Russell's MacReady in *The Thing*, other than perhaps the thick beard, it's possible to regard the character as much less affected by the magnetic or gravitational pull that the Thing exerts when compared to others in the film, a force that seems to bind all of them together in a state of physical and psychological homogeneity while leaving MacReady separated and apart. This conjoining of Thing victims begins with the personnel of the Norwegian base; we see them briefly as a group in the found video footage forming an unbroken ring around the crater that contains the crashed saucer, as though drawn to it, each man like a magnetised link in a chain. The Split-Face Thing that is also brought back to Outpost 31 appears to be a fusion of two people – Matthijs van Heijningen Jr.'s 2011 prequel confirms this – presenting a horrifically amalgamated 'Siamese twins' corruption of the classical Greek theatrical comedy/tragedy masks.

The team come face to face with the find from the Norwegian base.

When we see the Split-Face Thing bundle carried from the helicopter to the interior of the American base by a huddled surround of men, MacReady isn't one of them; he stays close to his vehicle while the group almost reverentially carry the 'body' away from it, the dark tarpaulin suggesting an inverted corruption of the white shroud used to carry Christ into the tomb. Once the bundle is inside and its contents revealed we see MacReady standing alone at the head(s) of the find, and while the others congregate around the operating table to look at it MacReady is instead looking at *them*. Blair's hacking autopsy of the mass of Kennel-Thing that they retrieve and his subsequent hypothesis clearly illustrates the compounding gather effect of the organism. As with the earlier Split-Face Thing reveal, one gets the impression that while Blair speculates the men are subject to the tension between repulsion and curiosity and as a result are almost being pulled towards the grotesque mangle of flesh, all except MacReady who appears to remain the furthest away.

Throughout the rest of the film there are several more allusions to MacReady's individuality and the others' herd assimilation. 'Mac's Shack', the small out-building where the pilot holes up with his J&B to play computer chess, locates him apart from the others from the outset. At a point in the film when suspicions are rife, when Nauls re-enters the main base having gone to the shack with MacReady to find out why the light had been switched on, the base cook tells the others that he has cut MacReady loose from the guide rope that links all of the base's buildings, thereby leaving MacReady unattached and at the mercy of the storm. When MacReady manages to get back into the base via the supply room and Norris and Nauls attempt to bring him down they fail to get a grip on him, like magnets failing to attach to a non-magnetic surface. The couch in the rec room twice serves as place of restraint, first when Copper, Garry and Clark are the prime suspects and later when MacReady conducts his hot needle blood test, and in each case several of the men are tied together in close physical contact with MacReady at a distance.

One of the more thoughtful inclusions in the 2011 *Thing* prequel is the evidence that the Thing is unable to assimilate metallic material, as demonstrated by the collection of dental fillings found in a shower cubicle and the disappearance of one character's earring. Although this isn't used as an explicit Thing characteristic or plot development in the Carpenter film there are several instances of the men at the base, other than MacReady, noticeably failing to keep hold of metal objects, as though even pre-assimilation they are experiencing the effects of the Thing's anomalous magnetism.

There's a subtle example of this when Windows comes across the Bennings-Thing mid-assimilation; just before running from the room it's possible to hear him drop a set of keys out of frame that we've previously seen him handling.[4] When panic kicks in after the blood in the freezer is tampered with we see first Garry relinquish his Colt Trooper revolver then Clark give up his flick knife, both of which end of up in MacReady's hands.

Clark has a final epic fail when attempting to stab MacReady with a scalpel which falls from his grip when he is shot. After firing off rounds at the men Blair succumbs to the movie cliché of throwing his empty-chambered gun at them when he's cornered in the radio room. Butterfingers Dr. Copper 'drops' the defibrillator pads into the Norris-Thing's chest cavity (and then some) and Fuchs' charred remains are identified by the metal spectacle frames that have fallen from him onto the snow.

By contrast MacReady manages to keep a hold of most things metal, handy when he's conducting the hot needle blood test obviously, and even when objects fail him or fall from his fingers he's able to regain control swiftly, such as when his flame thrower temporarily refuses to ignite in order to dispatch the Palmer-Thing or at the end when he manages to retrieve the puttering stick of dynamite that he drops in the tunnel and blow up the Blair-Thing. The latter is an interesting reversal of the fate of the Norwegian at the film's beginning who drops a thermite grenade into the snow but fails to retrieve it in time. Thermite is a pyrotechnic composition of a metal powder and a metal oxide, and clearly something that needs to be handled with care, which is difficult when you have Thing magnetism pulling it from your grasp.

So it seems that anything Thing-influenced is apt to disobey the laws of physics. This is especially apparent when one considers the behaviour of the organism in relation to gravity, which brings us back to the significance of the south polar setting. The Earth's magnetic field is subject to a phenomenon known as geomagnetic reversal, which in layman's terms involves an interchange in the position of magnetic north and magnetic south, a flip-flop that gets recorded in the minerals of sedimentary deposits and volcanic lava flows. This doesn't happen very often; the most recent occurrence is thought to have taken place around 780,000 years ago although it numbered among the many 2012 doomsday theories which, had it come to pass, would have denied you the opportunity to read this book.

The mere theoretical possibility of a world turned upside down, at least geomagnetically speaking, resonates in The Thing. The organism's anomalous relationship with the up/down rules of gravity are plain for all to see. Something clearly burst upwards and out of the block of ice the Norwegians took back to their base. A large piece of the Kennel-Thing appears to rise up and out through the rafters of the compound practically unaided. The Norris-Thing's gut-busting arachno-vermiform manifestation projects upwards and clings to the medical bay ceiling, while the Spider-Head bit of the Norris-Thing is conspicuously upside down, its world turned quite literally on its head. The Palmer-Thing's blood jumps up and out of the Petri dish in its attempt to escape the hot needle and then proceeds to run off along the floor of the rec room in a direction of its own choosing almost as though attracted to a magnetic source, while the Palmer-Thing itself performs a bizarre flip up to the rec room ceiling before descending and attempting to devour Windows. At the end the Blair-Thing rises up from beneath the base to threaten MacReady, propelling itself up through the floor with an inhuman strength.

The Thing at large in a world turned upside down.

The Thing effect, if you will, is that of polarisation. Sociologically speaking this is evident in the division and extremity that it brings to the men of Outpost 31. Overall it is responsible for a situation in which, despite appearances, everything is opposite to the known order. The threat to life emerges from inside to outside and, having emerged, refuses to observe the rules that distinguish up from down, black from white, right from wrong, human from alien.

Despite his admiration for the work of Howard Hawks, Carpenter, in electing to return to the core of the Campbell Jr. novella, flipped many of the changes that Hawks put in place with *The Thing from Another World*. Many of Hawks' films can be catalogued as 'base under siege' scenarios in which male bonding prevails and the concept of the group as an organic force pulling together for the greater good is expounded; the plots of many Hawks films such as *The Criminal Code* (1931), *Only Angels Have Wings* (1939), *Rio Bravo* (1959) and *El Dorado* (1966), not to mention *The Thing from Another World*, all bear this out. Carpenter's own *Assault on Precinct 13* (1976) is a direct homage to this Hawks blueprint. But his version of *The Thing* takes the convention and eviscerates it. Blair's autopsy of the Split-Face Thing, in which he cuts open the monstrosity and systematically removes and lists the heart, lungs, kidneys, liver and intestines, encapsulates Carpenter's conscious attempt to pull the organic group from the inside out and have it exposed to the open, a physical shift from harmony to disarray.

The monster in the Hawks film is typified as an external alien threat to the internal status quo. In the Carpenter film we are witness to the organism inveigling its way in and violently exploding back out. In so doing the ultimate result is a disruption of and an ambiguation between the notions of inside and outside. If one examines the remains of the buildings that form the Norwegian base and Outpost 31[5] the evidence points to a force that, once introduced, has ripped both apart in its attempt to move from interior to exterior, much like the effect the organism has on the bodies of the men it assimilates. What is left is a blurred state, where internal icicles hang down from the Norwegian ceilings and where we can expect the fires of Outpost 31 to be extinguished by the biting wind and drifting snow of the encroaching Antarctic winter...

'WHAT IS THAT... IS THAT A MAN IN THERE... OR SOMETHING?'

'Man', as the Carpenter film's most well-known tagline would have us understand 'is the warmest place to hide'. Despite the surface emphasis placed on the grotesque transformations it is the Thing in human form that is ultimately the greatest instigator of fear, for without the apparent physical normality that the assimilated men present we would not have the worried anticipation of eruptive abnormality spilling out violently before our eyes. Simply not knowing who is who, but knowing what happens when a Thing hidden inside a man decides that it's show time is the sublimely queasy key to the film's suspenseful, horrific effectiveness.

Apart from relocating his version back from the North to the South Pole, returning to the Campbell novella's hidden alien enemy motif was Carpenter's single greatest break away from the popularly accepted cinematic conventions set down by the Hawks/Nyby interpretation in 1951. How best to describe their monster? Let's take our cue from Ned 'Scotty' Scott (Douglas Spencer), the 'Tell Me, Professor' journalist who has tagged along with the crew dispatched to the US Arctic base Polar Expedition Six to investigate the find under the ice. After listening to an explanation of what the Thing is delivered by Dr. Carrington (Robert Cornthwaite), the 'As You Know, Bob' scientist[6] and apologist for the monster, Scotty exclaims 'an intellectual carrot – the mind boggles!' Essentially humanoid in shape, the Hawks/Nyby Thing has a head reminiscent of the Universal Pictures horror cycle's interpretation of Frankenstein's Monster. It subsists on blood and reproduces asexually by depositing seedlings. The Thing in the Campbell Jr. novella is described as possessing 'three mad, hate-filled eyes [that] blazed with a living fire, bright as fresh-spilled blood, from a face ringed with a writhing, loathsome nest of worms, blue, mobile worms that crawled where hair should grow' – so the bipedal taproot in The Thing from Another World is, to say the least, a departure from the source.

This deviation from the Campbell Jr. creation was possibly the first occurrence of a plant-based monster on the big screen, a sub-genre tendril that crept among the vegetable patch of modest budget horror/science fiction films for many years. The alien pea pods of Invasion of the Body Snatchers (Don Siegel, 1956) are arguably the pick of the crop with Steve Sekely's rather unfaithful adaptation of The Day of the

'An intellectual carrot!' James Arness as the titular thing.

Triffids (1962) offering a creeping, stinging asparagus/orchid mash-up as its threat to humankind. Roger Corman propagated some cuttings and came up with what can best be described as a Venusian crab-marrow in *It Conquered the World* (1956) but followed it up more memorably with the butterwort/venus fly-trap hybrid in *The Little Shop of Horrors* (1960). By the 1970s the vegetable invaders were consigned to spoof and parody, finding their nadir in *Attack of the Killer Tomatoes* (John DeBello, 1978) and its numerous wilting offshoots. One other film worth mentioning is *Matango* (Ishirô Honda, 1963), AKA *Attack of the Mushroom People* AKA *Fungus of Terror*, which has kitsch cult written all over it but was in fact based on a short story by the Edwardian supernatural horror writer William Hope Hodgson called *The Voice in the Night*. Hodgson's work had influence on the tales of H.P. Lovecraft, who contributed a short story to *Weird Tales* in 1930 entitled *The Whisperer in Darkness*, which featured the Mi-Go, a race of fungoid creatures.

The Hawks/Nyby frozen vegetable may have gone down well with audiences in the 1950s but twenty years after the release of *The Thing from Another World* John W. Campbell Jr. himself was still articulating his slightly less than rapturous response to the adaptation. In an interview for the book *Focus on the Science Fiction Film* (ed. William Johnson) he made this observation:

> They certainly changed it massively – but I've got to admit it was also certainly a highly successful movie. Maybe someday they'll try making my original story into a movie! ...I don't know why they considered it necessary to make the menace a

vegetable creature, instead of the entity capable of duplicating anyone it attacked so that not even his friends could tell he'd been killed and replaced. I believe my original idea would have made for far greater suspense. (Campbell Jr. / Johnson, 1972: 153)

There are only a couple of spurious nods given in the Carpenter film to the possibility that the Thing might be part-plant; the weird 'flower' that erupts from the Kennel-Thing to menace the men (an effect that special make-up effects creator and designer Rob Bottin referred to as the 'pissed-off cabbage', which is actually intended to be a piece of Thing formed of several dog-tongue copies) and the drawn-out green strings of vascular tissue that connect the assimilated Norris' head to his body when it decides that it's time to detach itself.

While much is made of the ways in which Hawks and Nyby diverged from the novella it does retain certain aspects that the Carpenter film, for all its efforts to return to the source, does not explicitly adhere to. There is direct unequivocal reference early on to the magnetic effect that the crashed saucer possesses; it causes the radio compass on board the crew's plane to behave oddly and the station's magnetometer records deviations originating from the crash site. More is made of the effect on the men required to stand guard over the Thing; Barnes (William Self), having inadvertently helped to thaw the creature out, is thrown into an extended funk at the sight of it, and two others guarding the greenhouse where the Thing has previously gained entry to the station are found hanging upside down from a beam with their throats cut. There may have been something in Campbell Jr.'s own underlying politics that chimed with Hawks' worldview. Campbell Jr. was well known for penning some highly opinionated editorials for *Astounding Science-Fiction*, repeatedly playing devil's advocate on the sensitive subject of race. Hawks maintained throughout his career that he was apolitical but his work was defined by a glorification of war (or at least its foot soldiers), the suppression of Native Americans, and an appetite for all-round manly huntin', shootin' and fishin'. The final defeat of the Thing at the hands of men in both *Who Goes There?* and *The Thing from Another World* unites the two and distinguishes them from the likelihood of defeat that the Carpenter film advances.

Going back to the tagline for *The Thing*, we may read the use of the word 'man' as shorthand for 'mankind' insofar as Blair's statistical extrapolations suggest a rapid and complete subsuming of all human life on Earth should the organism be allowed to reach civilisation. That singular 'man', though, is also effective in establishing a heightened sense of isolation. The Hawks/Nyby film was very much concerned with the reassuring plurality of 'men'. The poster taglines for the earlier film weren't exactly the stuff of legend; take your pick from 'Look Out, It's...', 'Howard Hawks' Astounding Movie' or 'Where Did It Come From? How Did It Get Here? WHAT IS IT?' Note however that the last question is '*what* is it?', not '*who* is it?', and certainly not the same as '*who* goes there?' The intellectual carrot was intended to be an objectified outsider, an embodiment of non-American otherness at a time of heightened fears of Communism in the United States. Flying out from Anchorage, the Americans head for a polar station close to the Distant Early Warning (DEW) line. We've already been told that the Russians are 'all over the pole like flies', so a Cold War frontier retread of a typical Hawksian Western is set up; the Soviets, the Sioux, the Thing – pick your 'Other'.

The Carpenter film wasn't alone in recapitulating 1950s science fiction/horror crossovers through a more jaundiced lens; remakes of *Invasion of the Body Snatchers* (Philip Kaufman, 1978), *Invaders From Mars* (Tobe Hooper, 1986), *The Fly* (David Cronenberg, 1986) and *The Blob* (Chuck Russell, 1988) all strove to reinvent or reinterpret the message behind the original films with varying degrees of success. The 1951 and 1982 *Thing* films, however, provide especially intriguing bookends to the Cold War. The Hawks/Nyby film was released some five years after the delivery of the Truman Doctrine, the announcement to Congress that is now widely recognised as the starting point of the era. The Carpenter film appeared just a few years before Perestroika, Tiananmen Square and the toppling of the Berlin Wall. Both came in the wake of a warmer war. In the Hawks/Nyby film the old bonds of World War Two combat camaraderie show themselves and are strengthened through a unifying mistrust of Atomic Age science. There's a reference to Bikini Atoll, site of 23 nuclear weapon tests between 1946 and 1958 and a psychocultural epicentre for the American public's developing mistrust of science and its hand in the business of mass destruction. We learn that Dr. Carrington has worked on the Bikini test programme, which immediately marks him as suspect in the minds of the film's original intended audience, and that's even before he's been seen on screen. His pointed beard, fur hat and effete (asexual?) demeanour leave no room for doubt that he is intended to be received as a potential Communist sympathiser. Inevitably it is he who seeks to protect the Thing, but his scheme is defeated by the combined efforts of Uncle Sam's boys. The team is led by no-nonsense, two-fisted Captain Hendry (Kenneth Tobey) whose patriotic anti-intellectualism (as opposed to intellectualism, be it Communist- or carrot-originated) results in the wanton destruction of the first recorded extra-terrestrial craft and the protracted and fatal electrocution of its one surviving inhabitant. Other scientists in the party elect to go along with Hendry's approach and help to bring about the demise of the monster, so the film's message is not exclusively anti-science. Rather, it portrays Carrington as driven by obsessive irrationality and science as put to best use when tempered by the rational and frankly xenophobic pragmatism that Hendry possesses. There is no doubt that it is the military who the audience is encouraged to regard as the decisive heroes.

The Carpenter film, in both harking back to the paranoia of the Campbell Jr. novella and moving beyond the Hawksian 'Band of Brothers at the O.K. Corral' formula, comes preloaded with post-Vietnam, post-Watergate, post-Operation Eagle Claw anxieties about American collective identity. [7] Unlike the men of Polar Expedition Six, the twelve individuals that share the confines of Outpost 31 are infused with ennui from the outset. The air of dysfunctionality and mistrust of authority is encapsulated in the character of Palmer, the pot-smoking pilot, who seems intent on sitting out his contract at the base watching reruns of TV game shows and whose early interactions seem driven purely by an effort to provoke and undermine what passes for the command hierarchy. His baiting of station manager Garry - 'I was wonderin' when El Capitan was gonna get a chance to use his popgun' – comes at an early stage and sets the tone for the blurring of authority that will follow. Garry is the nearest thing to a law man at Outpost 31, and his ridicule serves to illustrate Carpenter's intended overturning of Hawks' Western movie blueprint. When Garry surrenders his revolver midway through the film he may as well be placing his Sheriff's badge in the palm of MacReady's hand.

The ridiculously oversized hat that MacReady wears when piloting his helicopter apes not only Western movie traditions but is also a corruption of American military attire. The design is based on the classic US Army 'Campaign Hat' popular in the early 1900s, with its 'Montana Peek' and wide brim. One could also read that hat as a foreshadowing of the mutation of form that will affect the living later in the film. There are other props suggestive of war anxieties; the repeatedly-used M2A1-7 flamethrower, deployed extensively by US troops in Vietnam, is only partially successful at stopping the Thing. MacReady's flamethrower suffers temporary combat performance anxiety when he is faced with the Palmer-Thing. The sight of crashed helicopter wreckage, not unlike the flaming, smoking remains of the exploded Norwegian aircraft, became another symbol of the failure in Vietnam; according to figures found on the website of the veteran-run Vietnam Helicopter Pilots Association 11,827 helicopters were put to use by US forces during the conflict, of which 5,086 were lost.

MacReady's cassette recorder is an echo of Watergate; when committing his thoughts to tape for some supposed posterity he initially reports that 'nobody trusts anybody now' but chooses to edit out this thought by rewinding and recording 'nothing else I can do, just wait' over the top. It's an act that is perhaps contrary to MacReady's other character traits; why would somebody who is otherwise more than happy to express himself forcefully choose to edit himself in this way? His motivation could simply be the unalloyed mistrust that pervades the station – if the others were to hear about his trust issues they may use it as a reason to turn on him – although it's more likely a small plot device to signal the start of period in the film when the audience is invited to temporarily question the character's integrity. More on this later.

The Body Horror sub-genre that took off in the 1970s and arguably reached the height of its expression in the early- to mid-1980s correlates to the experiences of service personnel returning from the South East Asian theatre of battle and the reception of the images of war back in the US. The Thing can be read as Carpenter's most striking summation of the draft generation's countercultural *zeitgeist*, although it must go down as a late entry. Coming in the wake of *Dark Star* (1974) with its crew of apathetic, bearded space drop-outs, *Assault on Precinct 13* with its band of racially diverse, dispossessed individuals surrounded by a nameless, faceless enemy that, despite its losses, keeps on attacking and *Escape from New York* (1981) with its central character of Snake Plissken, a former Special Forces operative and heroic veteran of World War III turned criminal, it wasn't Carpenter's first look into that particular pit of paranoid despair.

There is something in the physical nature of the Things in his film that bears comparison with many of the images that emerged from the conflict in Vietnam; the My Lai massacre photography of Ronald Haeberle for example, especially 'And babies', the shot that became the image used in the iconic anti-Vietnam poster showing mangles of scattered, bloodied Vietnamese corpses, became etched in the American public's response to the hostilities. The flame-flayed Split-Face Thing found at the Norwegian base, with its fused contortion of appendages and twisted, frozen expression of horrific pain, is shot from angles that make it look remarkably similar to those casualties of war. Beyond the gross physical aspect the very notion of the Carpenter Thing presents a threat from an unseen and relentless enemy, one that springs back to life having seemingly been destroyed and plays a game of hide and seek that makes victory over it impossible, all of which could sum up the reality of the Viet Cong as experienced by American soldiers.

The remains at the Norwegian camp: an echo of Vietnam.

The differing gender politics that play out in the two films offer a further means of delineation. The so-called Hawksian Woman was an archetype coined to describe the ballsy, up-front female characters found in numerous Hawks films, typified by Katharine Hepburn in *Bringing Up Baby* (1938), Rosalind Russell in *His Girl Friday* (1940) and Lauren Bacall in *To Have and Have Not* (1944). In comparison to these sassy, confident women Nikki, the single female character in *The Thing from Another World* played by Margaret Sheridan, is, on the surface at least, relegated to the role of Hendry's love interest, present simply to prove that the captain is a red blooded male in order to distinguish him from the sexually ambiguous Carrington and the inhuman asexual Thing.

Other than that she appears to function primarily for much of the film as note-taker and coffee gopher while the men do all the thinking and acting. Beyond this initial impression however Nikki is arguably even more of an early screen feminist than the characters portrayed by Hepburn, Russell and Bacall. There are subtle points in her first scene with Hendry that establish her credentials; she and Hendry have had recent pre-marital sex which she had at least equal billing in instigating, before which she out-drank him. Not only that, we learn that she chose to broadcast their liaison to Hendry's Air Force colleagues. She even playfully feminises Hendry and exposes the extent of their intimacy by declaring 'well, your legs aren't very pretty'. Later on she jokingly invites Hendry to take a swing at her chin, contemplates asking him to marry her, goes in first for a kiss and even ties Hendry to a chair in order to tease him. All of this was, for 1951, remarkably transgressive, but because her character is developed through dialogue that is tonally *unremarkable*, unlike some of Hawks' more outspoken screen females, Nikki is not widely acknowledged as advancing the cause.

Ever the Hawks disciple, Carpenter regularly resurrected the Hawksian Woman model in his own films; certainly the two characters played by Adrienne Barbeau, Carpenter's one-time spouse, in *The Fog* (1980) and *Escape from New York* fit the archetype, as did Karen Allen's character in his later alien contact film, *Starman* (1984). In *The Thing*, however, there is a complete absence of female characters, save for MacReady's Chess Wizard computer (voiced by Barbeau), heard briefly in the opening few minutes of the film. The total lack of flesh and blood females further defines Carpenter's film as opposite to the Hawks film's frontier spirit; there's no option to procreate and expand, indeed the situation facing the men of Outpost 31 is one of contraction and ultimately hibernation. The only thing procreating and expanding is *the* Thing, as MacReady's final 'go forth and multiply' riposte to the Blair-Thing parodies. The smoky-voiced Chess Wizard machine is made to pay for its victory over the hirsute pilot when he pours a glass of J&B, ice cubes and all, into its innards resulting in a small shower of sparks. It's an act that mirrors the fate of the Blair-Thing at the film's end. Just like the Chess Wizard, the Blair-Thing pays for playing an aggressive winning move and is dispatched with a stick of dynamite, another act of sparking, explosive destruction delivered by MacReady. His boozy cut-the-bullshit counter strike in response to Chess Wizard's check mate move economically sets up his character; he's a game-changer ready to wield Occam's razor when faced with a challenge, a man with an illiberal attitude towards opposites. His 'conversation' with the chess computer, constituting the lines , 'poor baby, you're startin' to lose it, aren't ya?' and 'cheatin' bitch', points to a chauvinistic, intolerant personality type, somebody who destroys that which seeks to defeat him.

The Thing organism appears to be biologically non-gender-specific. By its very nature we can see that it is certainly non-*species*-specific. Essentially it works with whatever source of organic tissue it comes into contact with. However one can certainly read instances in its embodiment of the Monstrous-Feminine, an interpretation applied to horror cinema put forward by Barbara Creed in her book *The Monstrous-Feminine: Film, Feminism, Psychoanalysis*. Creed applied Freudian/Lacanian theory that relates female monstrosity to castration anxiety with the work of Julia Kristeva who considered it to be linked to fears of the reproductive function and association of the feminine with the corporeal. Creed identified examples of the 'castrating mother' in the themes and imagery of many horror films, from vampire movies such as *The Hunger* (Tony Scott, 1983) to female revenge stories like *I Spit on Your Grave* through to Norman Bates' avenging mother in *Psycho* (Alfred Hitchcock, 1960).

Creed paid particular attention to *Alien*, a film that is essentially one long tracking shot through a dangerous birth canal with countless womb images and maternal references. It's a film that starts with an entrance into the corridors of the *mother* ship Nostromo, equipped with an onboard computer called Mother, and ends with Ripley (Sigourney Weaver) expelling the alien from a narrow hatch in Nostromo's shuttle craft. The initial 'birth' of the alien, punching its way out of the stomach of Nostromo crewman Kane (John Hurt), closely resembles *The Thing*'s centrepiece sequence, the emergence of the Norris-Thing. In some respects the Norris-Thing sequence even more closely fulfils Creed's principle; not only do we have Norris' abdomen opening up to reveal a huge, ghastly orifice, the savage teeth that emerge around the perimeter of the cavity 'castrate' Dr. Copper's penetrating forearms and a grotesque ossified parody of Norris projects upwards out of the chomping maw to cling to the ceiling, dripping with viscous fluid. In her book Creed refers to this Thing manifestation as a creature:

> capable of cloning itself in the exact image of other life forms, as a gigantic organ with a large vaginal opening whose lips are peeled back to reveal a phallic-shaped bony

structure inside... a graphic representation of the infantile fantasy of the phallic mother who takes at least two forms, [one that] is thought either to possess an external penis or to have a penis hidden inside her body. (Creed, 1993: 50)

Not only does the Norris-Thing conform to this definition, it also references the phenomenon known as *couvade*, a part-biological, part-psychosomatic condition with its origin in the myth and ritual of many cultures around the world that involves sympathetic pregnancy symptoms in males. Monstrous life born of man as opposed to woman has taken many forms in horror cinema, usually as a result of some mad scientist giving birth to a horrific form of himself; for examples see all screen versions of Frankenstein, Dr. Jekyll and Mr. Hyde and the Wolfman through to the many birthing horrors to be found in the films of David Cronenberg such as *The Brood* (1976), *The Fly*

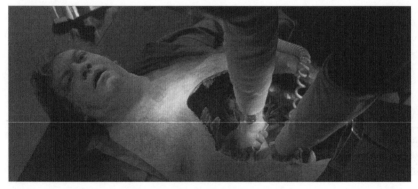

Copper up to his elbows in the Norris-Thing cavity.

and *Dead Ringers* (1988). Norris' chest pains and cardiac arrest become the labour pains before the 'birth' of the Norris-Thing, which delivers the *couvade* horror of man-as-mother with surreal shock and bloody immediacy. With this event, and several others in *The Thing*, there is an implicit sexualising of the alien otherness, because in a situation where there are only men present, that which is evidently not-men can be, must be, everything that is opposite. And so, amid all the churning flesh and disembodied howls and screams, each Thing eruption lends each man affected a violently feminised quality: Norris gives birth to the Norris-Thing; Palmer vibrates orgasmically before the Palmer-Thing bursts out, devouring Windows' (phallic) head with its freshly-torn and toothed head-gullet; the Blair-Thing sprouts dog-copies from its abdomen in some ghastly, self-mutilating mockery of a Caesarean section. Blair himself is shown hacking through the thick walls of a vast, uterine sac to deliver the part-copied dogs inside following the emergence of the Kennel-Thing.

One aspect that the Carpenter film does not show us is an embodiment that we can reliably regard as the original form of the Thing. This singles it out from all the other versions. We don't know exactly what the Norwegians found in the ice; all that can be deduced from the hollowed out block that MacReady and Copper find is its general dimensions. What we're provided with in the 2011 *Thing* prequel by way of a reveal is a disappointingly generic multi-tentacled black mass of alien-ness bursting from the block of ice. The very fact that we *don't* see the Iceblock-Thing in the 1982 film allows us to ponder what form it might have taken. We will pick up on this absence of form in the next chapter when discussing Carpenter's film-making techniques and creative choices, but it is worth noting now how important this lack of origin is to the notion of the Thing. In his analysis of the film for *The Cinema Book* (eds Pam Cook and Mieke Bernink), Michael Grant noted that:

> The lack of identity derives from the fact that when the entity manifests itself it reveals itself as always elsewhere, as unlocatable...*The Thing* seems to exist, if it can be said to exist at all, as a process of metamorphosis rather than as an entity with identifiable properties and qualities... what is crucial to the film is not so much the actions the station crew take in response to the Thing, but the Thing itself, or rather, the lack or absence it embodies. (Grant, 1999: 207)

Following this questionable origin further back we might also wonder if whatever crawled from the wreckage of the crashed saucer all those years ago was its pilot. This is one of those fan community imponderables, endlessly debated, never to be resolved. Perhaps it was the pilot, as was the case in *The Thing from Another World*, although it seems unlikely that it was the sole occupant of such a large spacecraft. So where are the rest of the crew? Perhaps, like the dog that makes it to Outpost 31, it was a surviving manifestation of the Thing organism that had infected the occupants of the saucer and entirely absorbed them. Sight unseen, it's interesting to imagine that, whatever form Carpenter's Iceblock-Thing took, it was a little bit of every life form the organism had previously come into contact with and assimilated, from every corner of the universe it had visited, like a well-travelled valise covered in exotic hotel stickers from around the world. For the purposes of building that all-important fear of the unknown, Carpenter portrayed the Thing as an astrobiological Swiss Army knife, capable of who knows what, being all things, so to speak, to all men. The grotesque twists and deformations of the flesh that we see reveal everything and yet nothing, as though on both a physical and metaphorical level the organism's contorted, amorphous embodiment relates back directly to the curious curves of that question mark at the end of *Who Goes There? The Thing from Another World* signs off with Scotty filing his report back to Anchorage via radio and ending with the warning 'Keep watching the skies!' If we could call out to the men of Outpost 31 in *The Thing* our warning would be to keep watching *each other*.

'WHAT THE HELL ARE YOU LOOKING AT ME LIKE THAT FOR?'

The eyes, as Cicero famously intimated, are the window to the soul. The appearance and also the covering up or absence of eyes formed an important part of John Carpenter's toolkit when making *The Thing*. New eyes frequently emerge out of the morass of convulsing Thing tissue, eyes that dart and probe the world that they have just been born into. They aren't looking to make eye contact, their purpose is more associated with seeking out an escape route. But if one's eyes should meet those of a Thing across a crowded room the 'soul' that they frame might just resemble the concentrated death throes of every being or beast that the organism has ever previously assimilated. The vile, seething aggregation of flesh that forms the Kennel-Thing appears to be teeming with large, rolling eyes. The Norris-Thing Spider-Head sprouts two eyes on stalks as part of its hasty attempt to regroup and scuttle off. The Palmer-Thing's eyes bulge and pop grotesquely when it starts to burst out of its human form. The eyes of the humans, real or Thing-copy, by comparison are frequently masked, by snow goggles or parka hoods, making it difficult for anyone – including us – to read them. Some of the group discussions between the men of Outpost 31 can feel like poker games; shaded eyes make it much harder to tell who's who or what anyone (or any Thing) is thinking.[8] When the Norwegian in pursuit of the dog during the film's opening scene is shot through the eye the brief sight of the fatal wound as the body lies in the rec room serves not only as a foretaste of the physical horrors to come but also suggests that the tell-tale fear in his eye has been extinguished, so that any clue as to the dangers of the dog have been shot through.

The camera under the control of a film-maker can be put to use as the 'eyes' of the intended audience. At a basic level the view might be intended to be read as the 'point-of-view' of the director, either literally or ideologically. In order to successfully suspend an audience's disbelief and draw them into a film's narrative a director needs to ensure that the viewer accepts the view that they are offered, identifying with whatever the camera is capturing and recording as if it were their own eyes. This assumes that an audience will passively receive and accept the director's preferred point of view. It doesn't really allow for each individual viewer's differing process of engagement with the visuals before

Who's who?

them. The theorist Christian Metz, in his book *The Imaginary Signifier: Psychoanalysis and the Cinema* suggested that the cinema screen possesses the qualities of a mirror; by identifying with the camera's 'gaze' a viewer is re-experiencing that important early stage of a person's development of self-awareness at which a mirror allows a child to regard itself as *other* existing within the world. So an engaging movie can provide an enveloping capsule of experience within which a viewer can temporarily adopt a provided view of the world. This facilitates an illusory sense of omnipotence, seeing all but not being seen.

The subjective point-of-view (POV) shot has been put to potent use in horror cinema many times; shots of victims-to-be have often been intercut with subjective POV shots showing the view of their approaching monstrous attacker, heightening the suspense and graphically capturing the terror on the victim's faces. The early film that used this most effectively was Rouben Mamoulian's 1932 *Dr. Jekyll and Mr. Hyde*. The film is full of such POV shots, allowing the viewer to get a sense of the subjective view of the central character(s) interacting with those around them. The same 'killer's eye view' effect was successfully reused in much later productions, prominent among which are Michael Powell's *Peeping Tom* (1960), albeit mediated via the lens of the killer's own cine camera, and John Carpenter's *Halloween*. Carpenter's regular cinematographer Dean Cundey made great use of the Panaglide, an early form of Steadicam camera, in the making of *Halloween*, especially for the opening shot through the eyes of the six-year-old Michael Myers as he sets about murdering his teenage sister. Among its many attributes, Steadicam technology allows for the smooth, seamless exploration of internal spaces, perfect for the director looking to build suspense and create an anxious thrill among audiences who will be rendered frightened by the thought of what might be lurking around the next corner. In the case of Michael Myers and that opening shot of *Halloween* we are gifted the added frisson of inhabiting the unbroken point-of-view of the young murderer, so that from the very outset, with no other POV conventions put in place, we are invited to see the world through his eyes and feel his motivation.

In the time between *Halloween* and *The Thing* Stanley Kubrick released *The Shining*, his brilliant, semi-faithful adaptation of the Stephen King novel. Anyone who has over-wintered at Amundsen-Scott South Pole Station will immediately link *The Thing* and *The Shining*; for many years the two films have been shown traditionally as a double bill for the station personnel to mark the departure of the last flight away from the continent before the weather closes in and the period of isolation from the outside world begins. But there are more ways to link the two films. Among its many glittering attributes, *The Shining* was a master class in camerawork within a controlled environment. The entirety of the Overlook Hotel, including the exterior snowbound maze steeped in salt and styrofoam, were all sets built at Pinewood and Elstree Studios.[9] These sets were an elaborate bagatelle for Kubrick to play with and another toy in the form of a specially adapted Steadicam, operated by its inventor Garrett Brown, provided him with the ideal means of capturing smooth, unbroken, controlled shots around the paths and corridors.

Aside from the probing corridor prowl of cameras around its confined studio-built sets, *The Thing* shares several other characteristics with *The Shining*; both play out in an isolated, wintry setting where the hostile conditions conspire against the protagonists and where links with the outside world (CB radio and snow cat in both cases) have been deliberately disabled; both reveal Man as Monster in the context of 'cabin fever' paranoia; and both portray an unstoppable process of the past repeating itself. Just as Jack Torrance (Jack Nicholson) seems destined to replay the murderous actions of the Overlook's former caretaker Grady as a result of unseen forces so the men of Outpost 31 seem powerless to avoid suffering the same fate as that which befell the Norwegians. The two films also offer their own interpretation on the concept of 'alienation', *The Shining* on a psychofamilial and spiritual/supernatural level, *The Thing* on a psychosocial and actual physical level.

The creepy exploration of internal spaces, or more specifically the use of an unreliable subjective camera, is what really links the two. In a 1996 article for the journal *La Licorne* Gaïd Girard identified why Kubrick's Steadicam footage following young Danny (Danny Lloyd) on his Big Wheel tricycle around the corridors of the Overlook works so well:

> The extremely low position of the camera and the amplified sound of the bike's wheels awaken in the spectator a feeling of malaise and of the unknown... Here, the image is read as coming from a subjective camera, but there is no imaginable subject. The camera's point of view thus becomes monstrous, dogging the little boy in an irrepresentable, menacing fashion. Who can see from that angle? The hotel? If so, does the Overlook then become a character? (Girard, 1996: 187)

Much the same can be said of Carpenter's pre-Kennel-Thing meanders around Outpost 31's interiors.[10] We have frequent low camera positions, arguably dog height although we can't say for sure that we're witnessing the point of view of the recently admitted Norwegian canine – just something not quite human. We're left with the feeling that some unseen agency is at large within the base and that we are sensing the spaces through its 'eyes'. There's an early slow gliding shot, just after Bennings, recently sutured from his gunshot wound, uses the intercom system to plead with Nauls in the kitchen to turn his music down. With the strains of Stevie Wonder's 'Superstition' still audible we cut to a head-height shot by the surgical lights in Medical which smoothly moves around the operating table, subtly lowers its view height and passes out through the door. There's a cut to a static shot of the empty rec room that is held for several seconds before a further cut to a darkened corridor. This shot also starts out held, static and empty until at the end of the corridor the Norwegian dog eventually appears and pads steadily forward before entering a room and, we have to assume, assimilating the room's one human occupant off-camera. This trio of shots, Medical to rec room to corridor, doesn't just build intrigue, it suggests through mood and restraint that with the dog allowed inside the base an unknown, indefinable presence has also entered. Much as we might unsettlingly come to think that our point of view following Danny around the Overlook in *The Shining* is that of 'Tony', his imaginary friend, showing the boy glimpses of the past or perhaps even the spirit of the hotel itself accompanying Danny, so we might suppose that our tour guide around the empty parts of Outpost 31 is something intangible and unearthly, there but not there.

Where the Thing isn't: Medical…

…rec room…

…corridor.

So whose or what's 'eyes' are we encouraged to imagine we are seeing through when the camera moves around the base? At times we are given the impression that our view could almost be that of a member of the base's personnel, albeit one who silently observes. There are several shots of the men grouped in a circle or semi-circle and we can choose to feel that our presence is somehow completing the ring. One might almost expect one or other of the characters to break into the heated discussion, look at the camera/us and ask 'so what do *you* think we should do?' By the time of these group discussions we might reasonably assume, as does MacReady, that one or more of the men in the group are no longer human. If therefore we are being encouraged through Carpenter's careful shot composition to imagine that we are observing events as though we are a member of a partially assimilated group, so we might amid the rising paranoia begin to wonder about our own humanity and ask ourselves a version of the question that Childs poses for MacReady during one of those round-robin discussions: if *I* was an imitation, a perfect imitation, how would I know if it was really me? We are immersed in the world of the film but are not of it, we feel present among the men but can only watch as their humanity or otherwise is revealed and wonder if this is what it feels like to have been assimilated, seeing all but not being seen – there but not there.

The Thing also shares with *The Shining* an underlying yet palpable impression of absence at the heart of its efforts to instil fear and suspense. In *The Shining*, apart from the largely depopulated hotel expanses, there is an emotional absence represented by the vacuum of love among the Torrance family members. In *The Thing* the absence, over and above the monster's lack of definable form, is embodied by the relative lack of visible human eyes and also in those shots of empty rooms and corridors. Carpenter is showing us where the Thing *isn't*; we're given just enough time to scan the rooms for signs of something, long enough to suggest that we're being shown these spaces for a reason, yet we find nothing and are left feeling unnerved. The length of time that a shot is held between cuts can help to increase that sense of unease, again a technique that both Kubrick and Carpenter used. In his book *Understanding Movies* Louis Giannetti defined the concept of the 'content curve', the point in a shot at which the audience might readily assume to have assimilated all of the information that they need in order to understand or make sense of what they are seeing and how this relates to their comprehension of the narrative. *The Shining* and *The Thing* are fine examples where the film-maker deliberately cuts either before or after the peak of the content curve. Cutting after the peak can seriously destabilise the viewer's experience, which is, of course, exactly what a horror director is seeking to do.

One area where the two films differ markedly is in their picture aspect ratio. Outside of a small number of projects, *2001: A Space Odyssey* (1968) being perhaps the most prominent example, Kubrick's films were shot for a 1.33:1 aspect ratio. *The Shining* was shot 'full frame' using the open matte technique which allowed him to take into account the standard American theatrical screen 1.85:1 framing ratio and also the then full screen 4:3 TV ratio when composing shots.[11] Almost without exception Carpenter shot his pictures in 2.35:1 widescreen anamorphic ratio, and *The Thing* provides clear evidence of his mastery of shot composition and editing within the widescreen format.

By the 1970s the use of the anamorphic ratio had come a long way from its beginnings as part of Hollywood's attempts in the 1950s to combat the rise of television. It took several years for its artistic merits and possibilities to be fully acknowledged, and many of the film industry's great names remained dead set against it in its early days. Fritz Lang famously summed up the pre-war generation of film-makers' attitude in a discussion of the merits of widescreen found during Jean-Luc Godard's 1963 film *Le Mépris*: 'Oh, it wasn't meant for human beings. Just for snakes—and funerals.' Orson Welles committed his thoughts to print on the oncoming tide of widescreen film processes back in 1958 in a piece published in the second International Film Annual. 'A film is a ribbon of dreams,' Welles waxed; 'It can happen to us to dream in colors and sometimes in black and white, but never in CinemaScope. We never wake from a nightmare shrieking because it has been in VistaVision.' His fixed belief in the poetic strictures of Academy ratio, the near-square picture format that he adopted from *Citizen Kane* onwards, was under pressure at that time, with Universal seeking to have *Touch Of Evil* (1958) shot in 1.85:1 VistaVision. Welles went on:

> A film is never really good unless the camera is an eye in the head of a poet... The camera is a means by which come to us messages from the other world and which let us into the great secret. This is the beginning of magic. But the charm cannot work unless the eye of the camera also is human. That eye should be on the scale of the human eye. (Welles, 1958: 250)

Carpenter's two main film-making heroes, Howard Hawks and Alfred Hitchcock, only shot one fully anamorphic widescreen picture between them. Although Hitchcock moved to 1.85:1 in the 1950s his was frequently a cinema of confinement which was not well-served by the extra picture width. In a 1956 Cahiers du Cinema interview intended to promote his one and only widescreen epic *The Land of the Pharaohs* (1956), and reprinted in English in the book *Interviews with Film Directors* edited by Andrew Sarris, Hawks had this to say about the format:

> We have spent a lifetime learning how to compel the public to concentrate on one single thing. Now we have something that works in exactly the opposite way, and I don't like it very much. I like CinemaScope for a picture such as *The Land of the Pharaohs*, where it can show things impossible otherwise, but I don't like it at all for the average story. Contrary to what some think, it is easier to shoot in CinemaScope – you don't have to bother about what you should show – everything's on the screen. I find that a bit clumsy. Above all in a motion picture, is the story. You cannot shoot a scene as quickly in CinemaScope, because if you develop a situation quickly, the characters jump all over the wide screen – which in a way makes them invisible. Thus you lose speed as a means of exciting or augmenting a scene's dramatic tension. (Hawks, 1956: 6)

While it is true that many early widescreen feature films were hamstrung by the apparent demands of the ratio, in the decades that followed plenty of directors proved that the increased width could be successfully put to use in the pursuit of creative breadth. Akira Kurosawa repeatedly demonstrated how to capture rapid movement amid compelling picture depth, David Lean was able to combine vast, epic landscapes with small, personal stories and Sergio Leone showed how to cut enveloping wide shots together with ultra-tight close-ups. The films of Nicholas Ray, Anthony Mann and Otto Preminger among others helped to further cement widescreen as a valid artistic choice. Carpenter's films have displayed all aspects of these earlier film-makers' methods and experience at one time or another. His work on *The Thing* is especially illustrative of his ability to meaningfully populate his widescreen compositions with an ensemble cast and combine both slow and rapid editing to heightened effect.

That range of cutting speeds was initially honed for use in interior set-based scenes on his Hawksian siege movie *Assault on Precinct 13*, a film that masterfully demonstrates the director's ability to confound the old preconception about widescreen being purely for spectacle not suspense. His multispeed editing gearbox was further augmented on *The Thing* by his decision to use a series of fade-outs and dissolves to connect some of the film's scenes. Several times, particularly in the first half of the film, scenes end on a freeze frame followed by a fade to black, but instead of a fade back in from the black screen the next scene cuts in immediately. Among a number of instances we see this happen at the end of Blair's autopsy of the Kennel-Thing and again when MacReady is taping his report on his cassette recorder. Fade-outs and fade-ins have come to be used as visual signifiers of the space between 'chapters' in the story of a film and a way to suggest the passage of time between scenes, neat indicators, if you will, of elapses that communicate the idea of 'later...'. The amount of time implied by the fade-outs in *The Thing* is ambiguous. They are certainly used to advance the story but it is frequently hard to tell just how much time has passed between scenes, particularly in the early stages of the film. It could be seconds, minutes or hours. There is something in the experiential effect of these unusual transitions that links in to the film's environment, allowing the viewer to feel the cold and become aware of the effort to retain clear-headed consciousness in a sub-zero climate and all the sensory confusion and sudden fear that that brings. It's almost as though the fade-outs to black represent the closing of our collective eyelids and shared cognitive capabilities and the immediate cuts to the next scenes are shouting 'wake up!'

Carpenter also uses several soft 'white-out' dissolves between some of the exterior scenes, notably when MacReady ponders the risks of flying to the Norwegian base in deteriorating weather conditions and later when he, Norris and Palmer visit the site of the crashed saucer and find the hole in the ice where the Norwegians cut out and kept the craft's sole survivor. Again these transitions help to neatly and economically nudge the plot along but also draw on environmental conditions to instil a hypothermic sensibility to the experience of watching the film; not that the director is trying to send us to sleep, more that he is lulling us so that the violence of the alien eruptions, when they come, is more shocking.

The Thing displays Carpenter's consummate ability to arrange his characters meaningfully within the frame, especially important for a film requiring numerous group shots set in environments and situations, such as the Antarctic exterior and station interior, that are less than conducive to the process of conveying identify and emphasis through character position. In the time since the publication of her BFI Modern Classics book on *The Thing* Anne Billson has revisited the film in various articles, and a 2012 posting on her blog 'Multiglom' picked up on this issue of group positioning, with particular reference to the scene in which Blair expounds his theory on the Thing to the assembled men in the wake of the Kennel-Thing emergence:

> This is a very important speech because it sets out the Thing's motivation and modus operandi, and the men don't just need to hear it, but need to be seen to be hearing it if the rest of the story is to make sense. The very elegant solution is for Blair to walk slowly around the carcass, explaining what he has discovered as he moves, while the men are shown listening to him, ever so slightly out of focus, in the near background… they all look as though they know what they're doing there – no-one is hovering around looking awkward or superfluous, and it doesn't strike you as peculiar that all these very strong, aggressive characters should shut up and let just one man talk... The arrangement of figures in the frame is maybe not the element that strikes you first when you watch *The Thing*, but it's as important to the overall success of the film as the screenplay, the performances and the special effects. Beautifully done. (Billson, 2012)

Strongly related to this, the film also sees Carpenter observe a technique for attributing character emphasis within the framing and positioning of actors that Hitchcock was known to use. Although no great lover of the widescreen ratio, Hitchcock made effective use of whichever picture format he used when it came to marshalling his actors to imply meaning through their position in relation to other actors. There is plenty of evidence in the sphere of visual semiotics and its research literature to suggest that significance can be attached to the area within an image where an artist or film-maker places people and objects. This relates in part to the Golden Section, the geometric rule of ratio that can be applied to images resulting in an aesthetically balanced and satisfying composition which emerged in the days of Pythagoras and

Euclid and has been observed by artists from da Vinci to Dali. It also relates, perhaps particularly when considering film over other visual media, to the principle of saccadic patterns. Saccades are the involuntary lightspeed-fast micro-movements of the eye when confronted with an image that enable the viewer to make sense of or capture meaning in the image.

A very basic example of this occurs in that famous perceptual illusion, often attributed to the British cartoonist W.E. Hill, that depicts either a young, beautiful 'wife' turning her head away or an old, ugly 'mother-in-law' with a large nose and chin, depending how you look at it. We are able to switch between the two in an instant because our eyes and brains work together to automatically apply either 'reading' of the image. The natural scanning patterns of saccadic eye movements are thought to explain the tendency in the majority of written languages and cultures to read lines of text from left to right, a tendency that can also be applied to the 'reading' of moving images. Readers of Arabic, Farsi, Hebrew or Urdu text, all of which share a tradition of being read right to left, may beg to differ with this observation. There's a whole other tome to be written about how this might be born out in the cinema of those cultures. Analysis of Hollywood cinema has certainly picked up on the tendency and used it to demonstrate why character position within the frame can be significant. For example Robert McKee, author of 'screenwriters' bible' *Story: Substance, Structure, Style and the Principles of Screenwriting* discussed *Casablanca* (Michael Curtiz, 1942) in a 1998 seminar, in particular the repeated positioning of Ilsa (Ingrid Bergman) on the right-hand side of the frame, to explain the part that left-to-right saccadic patterns play in establishing character traits:

> The left and right sides of a rectangular composition do not have the same emotional qualities. Objects on the right have psychologically a greater sense of weight, of power, of stability, of force, strength and solidity. Psychologically, a small object on the right actually balances a larger object on the left. A perfectly symmetrical composition leans to the right psychologically. He [Curtiz] puts her [Ilsa] on the right because he wants us to feel that this woman is the strength of this film. (McKee, 1998)

In *Understanding Movies* Louis Giannetti suggested that portions of visual compositions possess 'intrinsic weighting'. Put simply, characters placed on the right of the screen come across as stronger, more certain and more dependable than characters on the left, who are frequently portrayed as weaker or evil. Hitchcock's films are full of such instances; take the placing of Guy (Farley Granger) and Bruno (Robert Walker) in *Strangers on a Train* (1951) as an example. In a film that's all about the criss-cross swapping of roles, the visual formula of Guy: right side/good and Bruno: left side/ evil is established and then reversed at times when Guy's strength wavers and Bruno temporarily gains the upper hand.

Carpenter's framing of MacReady in *The Thing* substantiates this idea. Our first sight of him is in close-up playing computer chess in his shack armed with his trusty bottle of J&B. This is the first close-up shot of the film, which establishes MacReady as the main character who we might expect to be led to identify with the most. He is firmly on the right side of the picture looking left, his face illuminated by the computer screen. The last time we see him, almost the last shot of the film outside the burning remains of Outpost 31, he is in a very similar position, on the right side in close-up looking left, his face lit up by the flames, his bottle of J&B to hand. Topping and tailing his onscreen presence in this way might just help us to think 'this is R.J. MacReady, he started out human and he's still human'.

At other key points throughout the film MacReady figures on the right hand side of the picture. On the occasion of each Thing emergence that is where you'll find him, with the various Things holding the left 'evil' side: when the burned Kennel-Thing is extinguished MacReady is furthest right of frame holding a torch; when the Bennings-Thing is set alight he is right-side tipping up the canister of kerosene and igniting it with his flare; when the Norris-Thing puts in its appearance he is seen first on the right clutching a bundle of dynamite and holding the balance, then again when torching both the main body and the escaping head. His position for the final two emergences plays with this notion; when the Palmer-Thing emerges during the blood test scene MacReady is seen initially on the left side and all the while he is on the left he is unable to get his flamethrower to work. It is only when the angle of view changes and he is seen right of screen that his weapon sparks up and burns the monster. At the end when the Blair-Thing erupts from below MacReady is initially knocked off his feet causing him to drop the stick of dynamite. He cowers on the left as the Blair-Thing commands the right of the picture. When MacReady picks himself and the dynamite up, regaining the

MacReady on the right looking left: at the beginning...

...in the middle...

...and at the end.

initiative and disposing of the monster with his 'Fuck you too!' he is once again seen on the centre-right side of the screen.

There are a few other moments in the film where MacReady's position switches sides to suggest doubt as to his strength, confidence and humanity. These moments are within the section of the film when our perception of MacReady is challenged the most. When he is speaking into the microphone of his cassette recorder to record his audio diary we initially see him right of picture, but as he reveals his doubts in monologue the camera slow pans round to the right so that MacReady's position is more centre left. The final shot in the tape recorder scene shows MacReady from behind on the far left. In the very next scene, featuring Fuchs at work in the lab on tests to uncover who's human and who's Thing, we see MacReady framed and back-lit in the doorway behind Fuchs on the left of the picture, a possible nod to the well-remembered doorway-framed and silhouetted appearance of the Thing in the Hawks/Nyby film just before the men of the base in that film set it alight. Moments later, when we see Fuchs find some of MacReady's shredded garments in the snow, there's a cut from the stencilled name on the fabric to MacReady inside the base asking about Fuchs' whereabouts and ordering the other men around. During this scene he is once again centre-left or left of frame, and he remains so in the next scene when going out to check on Blair in the tool shed. Here again we see him framed left of picture within an entranceway, this time just his flare-illuminated face in the hatch of the tool shed door. Our temporary doubts as to his humanity lead importantly up to this scene as a means of maintaining our belief in Blair's authenticity, which of course proves to be misplaced.

The one word that frequently crops up in reviews of the film, both positive and negative, is 'visceral'. This might be in reference to the performances of the cast or the motivating impulses of the characters; certainly reason loses out to gut instinct and the raw emotional survival imperative once it's clear what the men are up against, and the likes of Kurt Russell and Keith David chew enough scenery during their nihilistically gutsy interpretations of their roles to warrant the term, thanks in huge measure to the close understanding that the actors had with their director. Russell and Carpenter especially are the last word in actor-director collaborations; Empire magazine put them at the very top of a list of forty such partnerships, above such notable couplings as Scorsese & De

MacReady's humanity in question: left, framed in a doorway...

...and left, framed through the tool shed door hatch.

Niro, Lean & Guinness and Burton & Depp. In the five films they have made together Carpenter has extracted some singularly tough, aggressive, non-conformist performances from the actor that would probably be defined by the pop culture cognoscenti as 'badass'. Of Snake Plissken, the character he has played twice, in *Escape from New York* and *Escape from LA* (1996), Russell himself has said '[he is] a visceral character, one that you feel, not that you figure out'. MacReady is cut from the same cloth as Plissken; anti-authority but perhaps the only one capable of and ready, albeit reluctantly, to take on the challenge at hand with his scratch-built 'cut the bullshit' approach to problem-solving.

The film's visceral nature also extends to its soundtrack. The legendary Ennio Morricone, credited with the score, lent a heartbeat motif to the aural experience, a darkly insistent pulsation that never quickens, suggesting an alien presence from the outset that is alive, calculating and prepared to take as long as it takes.[12] The music often lapses into a fixed landscape of fundamental tones, frequently centring on a monotone that can be felt as much as heard. The first Thing transformation scene is a case in point, and also shows the rewards of 'whatever works' film-making. *The Thing*'s co-producer Stuart Cohen tells the story on his excellent blog 'The Original Fan' dedicated to his memories of the film:

> When we played back the completed kennel sequence for the first time we looked at each other and shrugged. There was something missing – despite all the meticulous work the scene fell flat. Our salvation lay in a track our music editor, Clif Kohlweck, found at the last minute. The low drone sound that begins as MacReady and Co. slowly approach is a sound effect, actually background air conditioner hum sharpened, shaped, and eventually pushed to absurd levels before being taken out on the first shotgun blast. But what the hell, it worked, and the scene came alive. (Cohen, 2012)

Carpenter and his crew not only manipulated soundtrack and sound effect, they added an extra visceral edge through the vocal range of the characters, both human and Thing. The sounds that issue from each Thing are not only the screams of all that it has previously assimilated, they mix in the voices of those in the process of being assimilated. The tongues of victims are frequently silenced; Bennings is seen with a thick tentacle filling his mouth part-way through his death, Windows is struck dumb just before the Palmer-Thing tries to devour him and Garry's final screams are covered by the Blair-Thing's hand. It's often unclear exactly where the Thing's 'voice' emerges from. The first sign that the Kennel-Thing is about to appear is a disembodied hissing sound but this doesn't seem to be coming from the creature's mouth. Even more curiously, when MacReady tests the Palmer-Thing's blood it not only jumps up out of the Petri dish but also issues a high-pitched squeal. How can a liquid make a sound like that? As MacReady says, 'every little piece was an individual animal with a built-in desire to protect its own life'. When stung into action the blood sample screams in some alien approximation of pain, an escape of 'breath', for want of a better term, that is as much a signifier of the Thing's insides coming out as any of the sprouting viscera that famously splatter forth. Talking of which...

'WEIRD AND PISSED OFF WHATEVER IT IS'

'Body Horror' as a formal phrase didn't exist in cinema literature at the time of the making of *The Thing*. The term is widely considered to have been coined by the Australian writer and all-round creative polymath Philip Brophy in spring 1983 in an article published in the journal *Art & Text*, which was republished for a significantly wider audience in a special issue of *Screen* in January 1986. Brophy's single use of the specific term in the article actually came during his discussion of *The Thing*, which he regarded as Body Horror taken to its 'logical limit'. He went on:

> [It] deal[s] with the notion of an alien purely as a biological life force, whose blind motivation for survival is its only existence. Not just a parasite but a total consumer of any life form, a biological black-hole. The essential horror of *The Thing* was in the Thing's total disregard for and ignorance of the human body. To it, the human body is merely protein - no more... *The Thing* does not honour any of our beliefs or perceptions of what the human body is. (Brophy, 1986: 10)

Considering that this was written in the early 1980s amid the slew of poor reviews for *The Thing*, Brophy's high regard for the film and positioning of it as an exemplar of the sub-genre now seems prescient. His article suggests that at a point in the late 1970s the likes of Carpenter, George A. Romero, Ridley Scott and especially David Cronenberg sought to eschew the prevalent realism that had seemingly absorbed the horror genre since the hey-days of Universal, Hammer and Toho Studios and inject a fresh and frequently surreal viscerality. However his analysis overlooks the significance of a trio of films that predate the rise of Body Horror by some twenty years, namely *Eyes Without a Face* (*Les Yeux Sans Visage*) (Georges Franju, 1960), Powell's *Peeping Tom* and Hitchcock's *Psycho*, all of which explored the graphic puncturing of the fabric of bodies in ways previously unseen in cinema, thereby ventilating the formalities of horror cinema with their starkly forensic precision.

If one were to widen one's search for Body Horror's antecedents beyond filmic reference points and scrutinise the broader plain of twentieth century art and its reflection of the butchery of that century's conflicts, it would certainly be possible to see the influence of the work of painters such as George Grosz and Pablo Picasso from the period following World War I and that of Francis Bacon and Graham Sutherland in the wake of the 1939–45 hostilities. The bodily deformations and human-animal hybrid creations seen in the work of the French sculptor Germaine Richier, especially her post-World War II work, might also factor as an influence. One theorist, the art historian and critic James Elkins, hypothesised in his book *Pictures of the Body: Pain and Metamorphosis* that the horror represented by the externalised viscera of the monsters seen in *The Thing* can be traced back to creatures found in Greek and Babylonian myth, specifically the Gorgon, commonly epitomised by the three sisters Stheno, Euryale and Medusa, and Humbaba, 'Guardian of the Fortress of Intestines' slain by Gilgamesh.[13]

Humbaba, Guardian of the Forest of Intestines.

The original Monstrous Feminine, Gorgons have come to be regarded as an embodiment of deadly female sexuality; Sigmund Freud, no less, in his 1922 essay 'Das Medusenhaupt' ('The Head of Medusa') relates the snake-like hair and gaping mouth of the monster to an externalisation of the emasculating threat to man of the female genitalia. Quite apart from the castration anxiety that the Thing's various maws and jaws represent, its ability to silence its victims, rendering them mute, mesmerised and stiffly rooted to the spot at the point of attack as discussed in the previous chapter, bears some resemblance to Medusa's capacity for turning men to stone with one look. Added to which, the detachment of the Norris-Thing's head when the body is set alight by MacReady could also be thought of as a perverse reenactment of Medusa's decapitation by Perseus.

Perhaps as much as 700 years before the earliest records of Gorgons in Greek mythology, back to the first known tablets poetically relating The Epic of Gilgamesh, thought to date from the eighteenth century BC, Humbaba reared its very ugly head. The description suggests a creature that has a face made out of its own intestines, a single coil of entrails that form its features in repeated descriptions and representations, for which ongoing evisceration is life. The demigod Gilgamesh, fifth king of Uruk, kills Humbaba by pulling its 'insides' out, thus returning its exposed internal organs back to its interior, the normal state for mortals which brings death to the creature. Elkins draws comparisons between Humbaba's exoviscera and the Thing's gross externality during assimilation and emergence, inverted bodies that are violently and horrifically alive when not conforming to accepted anatomical orthodoxy.

For all this high-minded comparative conjecture it seems highly unlikely that the Special Make-up Effects Unit and production illustrators that worked on The Thing were terribly familiar with ancient Mesopotamian poetry and went looking for stone tablet depictions when researching the creature designs. There isn't a vast amount of published literature contemporaneous to the film's release to feature first-hand accounts of the design process, although quite a lot of light was shed in an extensive article printed in a special double issue of the magazine Cinefantastique dating from October 1982. This issue of the magazine is something of a bible for Thing aficionados; it's one of those publications, no matter how dog-eared (although ideally pristine and kept in a protective sleeve for safe presentation at occasional bragging rights ceremonies) that any self-respecting fan has to have in their collection. The magazine's 27-page article, written by David J. Hogan with additional interviews by Michael Mayo and Alan Jones, focuses primarily on the creation of the film's special effects and introduces four key players in this process: Dale Kuipers, Mentor Huebner, Mike Ploog and Rob Bottin.

In light of this scarcity of contemporary published accounts – other than the lengthy Cinefantastique piece there were some photo-heavy tidbits in magazines such as Fangoria and Starlog but that was about it – co-producer Stuart Cohen was kind enough to answer the call and share his thoughts on the production's influences for the benefit of the book that you're reading:

In thinking back about the initial design days I realise that EC Comics were a singular influence on all of us and a common departure point for discussion between John, Rob, Ploog, Mentor, myself, etc. There had recently been a well promoted revival, and they were easy to access for the first time in years (John kept newly published hardbound anthologies in his office). Much discussion centred around their boldness, the outsized sense of exaggeration inherent in their execution, particularly the idea of things coming directly at you. Although John and I occasionally talked about the influence of Lovecraft or Bierce ourselves, I don't remember there being much literary discussion with the group itself – I think there was some question of how much of this stuff Rob, at 22, had read. The pulp influence, if anything, is seen in Dale Kuiper's final design for the monster, which was also partially modelled after Bill Lancaster's original draft. The only movie I remember serving as any sort of reference point was *The Exorcist*, more in execution than design, with both John and Rob unified in their admiration for the work of Dick Smith. (Author's interview)

For the uninitiated, EC Comics started out in the 1940s producing illustrated science, history and bible stories for school children. When William M. Gaines, son of company's founder Max Gaines took over in 1949 he quickly switched the emphasis on to crime fiction, often dealing with social issues such as racism and drug abuse, and gritty, downbeat military fiction that was far removed from the post-war heroism prevalent in other contemporaneous publications. Gaines, a fan of H. P. Lovecraft among others, pushed his artists and writers to produce stories that were increasingly grim and gruesome in nature and by early 1950 EC was publishing the bi-monthly horror books *Tales from the Crypt*, *The Vault of Horror* and *The Haunt of Fear* for which it became renowned. These titles ran for four years before falling foul of the United States Senate Subcommittee on Juvenile Delinquency which practically put EC out of business. Gaines valiantly defended his publications before the committee, although EC's output was so defiantly swimming against the McCarthyite tide of the times that the fate of its horror titles seemed sealed. Gaines went down fighting though, as this exchange between him, Chief Counsel Herbert Beaser and Senator Estes Kefauver about the nature of some of his comics' cover illustrations testifies:

Mr. Beaser: Is there any limit you can think of that you would not put in a magazine because you thought a child should not see or read about it?

Mr. Gaines: My only limits are the bounds of good taste, what I consider good taste.

Sen. Kefauver: This seems to be a man with a bloody axe holding a woman's head up which has been severed from her body. Do you think that is in good taste?

Mr. Gaines: Yes, sir, I do, for the cover of a horror comic...

Sen. Kefauver: This is the July one. It seems to be a man with a woman in a boat and he is choking her to death with a crowbar. Is that in good taste?

Mr. Gaines: I think so.

(Senate Subcommittee on Juvenile Delinquency testimony transcript, 1954)

Gaines had the last laugh, literally, when from the EC ashes was raised the phenomenon that was *Mad* magazine, the hugely popular satirical title still published to this day. The period between 1950 to 1954 during which EC put out its most grisly comics is analogous to the period between 1930 and 1934 when Hollywood released a stream of frequently lurid and risqué entertainment before the Hays Code was established and a dark age of censorious decency prevailed. For a young John Carpenter, EC's grotesquery held an illicit appeal. In an interview with James Verniere for the November 1982 issue of *The Twilight Zone Magazine* Carpenter discussed his affection for them:

I loved EC Comics. But you see, my parents, my dad especially, felt concerned that all of this stuff was warping me very badly – movies, comic books. He wanted me to learn the violin and stuff like that. So of course it was partially because he didn't want me to do it that I did it. And EC Comics were the real forbidden fruit. I mean they were dangerous to the mind because they were so graphic. But they were also wonderful, so inventive. (Carpenter in Verniere, 1982:28)

His love of the horror comic has clearly stayed with him throughout his film-making career. As recently as 2011 Carpenter had a hand in creating a new magazine, *Asylum*, which paid homage to the grue of EC in its graphic depictions of retributive dismemberment and which boasted an anti-hero in the form of Beckett who bore a close resemblance to the sort of characters that Kurt Russell has played for the director so often. Leafing through an issue of an EC Comic now it's not hard to see echoes in the conceptual drawings that Carpenter's illustrators produced. Dale Kuipers was Carpenter's first choice concept artist, having been recommended by *The Thing*'s producers Larry Turman and David Foster who had worked with Kuipers on the moderately dreadful spoof *Caveman* (Carl Gottlieb, 1981). His initial sketches and ideas were very well received by Carpenter, although looking back one or two aspects were a little close in nature to the creature ideas found in Ridley Scott's *Alien*; for example, the Thing 'reproduction' would occur when a parasite would latch onto a victim's head and deposit eggs into the host's oesophagus. The stage was set for Kuipers to take on the film's creature design role, but a motorcycle accident that sidelined him for two months led to Carpenter approaching Bottin with whom he had worked on his earlier film, *The Fog*.

Bottin quickly assembled a more than 40-strong effects team comprising illustrators, designers, sculptors, painters and technicians and in the early stages worked closely with illustrators Mentor Huebner and Mike Ploog. Huebner's vast storyboarding and production art experience has encompassed over 250 films, from classics such as *Forbidden Planet* (Fred M. Wilcox, 1956), *Ben-Hur* (William Wyler, 1959), *North by Northwest* (Alfred Hitchcock, 1959) and *The Time Machine* (George Pal, 1960) to more recent landmarks such as *Blade Runner* (Ridley Scott, 1982), *Dune* (David Lynch, 1984) and *Bram Stoker's Dracula* (Francis Ford Coppola, 1992). His storyboard sketches, especially for the Kennel-Thing scene and the Blair-Thing climax, closely resemble the shot compositions and camera angles that found their way into Carpenter's finished film and so Huebner deserves considerable credit for informing the eventual mise-en-scène. Bottin worked even more closely with Ploog and it is arguably his artwork that most closely resembles the majority of the final creature manifestations. Prior to working on *The Thing*, Ploog built his reputation through comic books and is best known for his involvement with series such as *Man-Thing, Monster of Frankenstein* and *Ghost Rider*.

Ploog was actually on board the project about a month before Bottin was appointed but when the two came together the result was a perfect storm of ideas. Fanboy lore has it that Carpenter's words of creative direction to Bottin at the beginning of his involvement were 'Okay kid... go nuts!' Whatever the details of his instructions were, the resultant work became an all-consuming venture, a benchmark in special effects that would stretch the film's finances (the make-up effects budget swelled from an initial $750,000 to $1.5 million) and also its production schedule. Many times the actors are seen responding to monsters that at the time of shooting were either still being made or in some cases still being designed. Bottin's time on the film ran for 57 weeks, from April 1981 through to late May 1982. That's about three weeks before the film's scheduled release date, so quite a lot of the on-screen gloop was very fresh indeed. Ploog worked through until late 1981 but was committed to travelling to England to work on *Superman III* which is the point at which Huebner stepped in to complete the conceptual work with Bottin, principally the dog transformation sequence and the realisation of the Blair-Thing, both of which required further development.

The No.1 piece of fanboy lore about the film production process, which emerged in the *Cinefantastique* article, is that as a result of working round the clock seven days a week for over a year on the effects, Bottin was hospitalised with extreme exhaustion. It was towards the end of the second unit shooting schedule that the highly experienced Stan Winston was therefore called upon to contribute, and elements of the Kennel-Thing creation, including the effects component nicknamed the 'chicken-dog', is Winston's handiwork. This sequence, coming late in the production, seems to correspond with Bottin's health-enforced temporary absence. There is no doubt that the punishing schedule pushed Bottin to the boundaries of his physical well-being. What is perhaps less well known to anyone who hasn't read the *Cinefantastique* article is just how much the young effects designer's landmark work on the film would ruffle the feathers of the Make-up and Hair Stylists Guild, a wing of the International Alliance of the Theatrical Stage Employees (IATSE), the union that represents the crafts people in the entertainment industry and provides guaranteed basic wages, working conditions, healthcare and pension benefits. Universal were forced to pay out $10,000 in damages to IATSE who claimed Bottin's creations did not constitute 'make-up' and that by crediting him as 'special make-up effects creator and designer' the studio violated the alliance's collective bargaining agreement.

When questioned about these problems for the *Cinefantastique* article Bottin seemed relatively sanguine, but it's likely that, quite apart from the challenging physical aspects of the role, the little local difficulty with the unions added to the strain. Stuart Cohen again:

> When I think now about the environment Rob was working in, what I find most striking is how new, and therefore frightening to the production establishment, the whole enterprise was at the time. There was simply no template – creative, financial or otherwise – for what we were about to attempt. I was involved in the set-up of Rob's unit at Hartland [the sound stage in North Hollywood where Bottin was based] and it was almost impossible to convey to the various unions at the time who would be doing what. This meant, in addition to everything else heaped on his young shoulders, Rob was required to be a politician, enduring many pop 'inspections' from suspicious officials, for example, and having to deal with their thinly veiled enmity. With all this confusion and uncertainty, and with the pressure on (from John and others) to produce, it is in retrospect not hard to see why he ended up needing hospitalisation. (Author's interview)

Bottin's effects demonstrated an amazing ability to generate animacy from inanimacy. Into his mixing bowl went a huge range of ingredients. The various marionettes and armatures, packed with radio-controlled parts, air bladders, wires, hydraulics and pull cables, were subsumed beneath foam latex, fibreglass and rubber and then coated with just about any substance to hand that would do the job: KY Jelly, bubble gum, strawberry jam, mayonnaise, cream corn, gelatine and food thickener. Out of necessity Bottin's skills extended to growing a thicker skin of his own, one able to deflect the technical and industrial problems that beset his time on the production. He'd need that thick skin during and beyond the film's release. The disgruntlement of the unions probably led to a complete lack of acknowledgement from the Academy of Motion Picture Arts and Sciences when 1982's Oscar nominations were decided upon. Bottin would get one award nomination, for the Saturn Award for Best Special Effects presented by the Academy of Science Fiction, Fantasy & Horror Films, but he lost out to Carlo Rambaldi and Dennis Muren for their work on *E.T. The Extra-Terrestrial* (1982), one of the many trouncings that Steven Spielberg's cute alien would give Carpenter's creation. Rather incredibly Ennio Morricone's now-revered score received the film's only other award nomination: *Worst* Musical Score at the Golden Raspberry Awards, or Razzies for short, the anti-Oscars presented each year in recognition of the worst in film. It lost.

The Body Horror films of the 1980s craved one thing in particular: a reaction. Through their succession of evermore gruesome tableaux they sought to reveal images of arresting physical impossibility with the intention of provoking fright through sheer spectacle. With all of their comparatively advanced technical sleight of hand it can be argued that the makers of these films were striving for the same kind of response in their audiences as many of the pioneers of pre-cinema with their deliberately fright-inducing magic lantern shows. The films that emerged during the 1980s Body Horror cycle specialised in gruesome transformation sequences of one kind or another, which tended to be presented as extended visual party pieces. Frequently eating up a major part of the budget – *The Thing* was no exception with an eventual effects budget totalling one tenth of the overall production cost – the film's makers wanted to make sure their audiences really saw just what they had blown their budget on, and so often the effects sequences were given extended screen time, sometimes at the expense of the film's pacing. Take the transformation scenes in films like *An American Werewolf in London* (John Landis, 1981), *The Company of Wolves* (Neil Jordan, 1984) and *The Fly*. What these scenes share is a relative suspension of narrative momentum, as though everything stops so that the viewer can take a good look at the fine detail of what is happening.

The kinetic nature of the new make-up effects and animated mannequins practically demanded a halt to the plot flow so that they could take centre stage and be shot from a multitude of angles, often inter-cut with a series of suitably pop-eyed and open-mouthed reaction shots of actors seemingly rendered sclerotic with fear. It was blink-and-you-*won't*-miss-it horror. While many of these sequences were executed with great skill so as to ensure the results appeared convincing, they can seem curiously laboured to today's audiences well used to the hyperkinetic pixelated impossibilities of CGI. Looking back and comparing it to its Body Horror contemporaries, part of *The Thing*'s great alchemy is that, contrary to the prevailing view among critics in 1982, its parade of effects sequences conceived and fashioned by Bottin and his team neither interrupt nor dominate the beat of the film. In fact if anything they reflect and accentuate its confidently inexorable stride pattern. Carpenter wove them in to his same skilled process of shot composition, cutting, lighting and camera positioning as can be seen throughout the rest of the film.

Above and beyond the graphic extremity of the effects, and putting to one side the winning template set down by *E.T.* for the reception of cinematic alien life in 1982, perhaps this sequential frequency of effects in *The Thing* also told against the film when it was initially received by critics and audiences. The extent to which the tenacious regularity of gore upset the journalists' sensibilities is a matter of debate. It's quite likely that, however good Carpenter's film turned out, some of them were just too wedded to the Hawks/Nyby film to give a remake any credence. The fusillade of damning scorn that was unleashed by the critics is now pretty well documented in retrospective accounts of the film's life cycle. It will suffice to reprint just some of the choicest epithets here as an indicator of the tenor of the reaction (critics' names have been withheld to protect the embarrassed):

'a great barf-bag of a movie'

'a wretched excess'

'instant junk'

'atrocity for atrocity's sake'

'no subtext, no humour, no genre invention'

'foolish, depressing, overproduced'

'this is a film about tentacles and teeth and eyes and orifices and goo, goo, goo'

'so single-mindedly determined to keep you awake that it almost puts you to sleep'

'a mindlessly macho monster mash'

'Carpenter was never meant to direct science fiction horror movies. Here's some things he'd be better suited to direct: traffic accidents, train wrecks and public floggings.'

And it was not only those paid to appraise it who expressed their misgivings. After the film's first press screening, at Universal's Alfred Hitchcock Theatre on 11 June 1982, the film's veteran matte artist Albert Whitlock left Stuart Cohen in no doubt how he felt about it. This from Cohen's blog:

I was confronted in the lobby afterwards by a visibly angry Albert Whitlock, who thought the film was unnecessarily weighted toward gore and violence at the expense of almost everything else – he said his wife had to leave the theatre during the kennel scene and chose not to return. He found much of the film offensive, the first time I had heard this word used by someone closely connected with us to describe this movie. (Cohen, 2012)

Whitlock's highly negative reaction to the film is also recorded in the *Cinefantastique* article. In recalling a post-viewing conversation he'd had with Carpenter, he is quoted thus:

I told John it should have a new title: *Slaughterhouse-Six* [Whitlock had worked as matter supervisor on George Roy Hill's 1972 screen adaptation of the Kurt Vonnegut Jr. novel *Slaughterhouse-Five*]. I know that death is death, and that there are horrible things, but I don't have to go to the movies to see it. You use it as a theme, but you don't hit people on the head with it. (Cohen in Cinefantastique, 1982: 74)

Kurt Russell also expressed concerns after the press screening. He felt that much of the work that he and the rest of the cast had put into building up relationships between characters had been sacrificed in favour of what he referred to on the night as 'the ick factor'. Judging by his contribution to the film's DVD release feature commentary he's settled well into enthusiastic retrospective appreciation.

The press response in the days and weeks that followed can now be thought of as mere nesting material for the film's long, slow incubation. Unlike the organism in *The Thing* which Blair's calculations worked out would take 27,000 hours to infect the entire world population (which to save you doing the sums is a little over three years) it took years and years for the reappraisal process to occur. From the home video groundswell, through rather Johnny-come-lately academic acknowledgement, eventual journalistic enthusiasm and the burgeoning articulation of fan adoration courtesy of the internet, at each step *The Thing* has found fresh assessment that was increasingly positive and incisive.

With every new growth ring of reappreciation came the acid test reaction to the effects. Quite how people react to the film, even today when apparently gore-desensitised horror fans are seemingly able to sit through any amount of violently sadistic torture and bloodshed without registering much of a response, provides evidence to back up some interesting theorising. Reactions to horror films *per se* tend to take two diverging paths; one moves off in the direction of covering one's eyes, expressing a desire to stop watching or leave the viewing environment and leading, in extreme cases (if you believe the frequently manufactured word-of-mouth marketing around some films), to vomiting, passing out and religious conversion. The other takes a direction of response that is closer in nature to the pleasure that theme park ride junkies derive from the thrills and spills of the roller-coaster experience. Not only are they able to tolerate the wanton ghastliness, they seem to positively *enjoy* it.

The authors of a 2008 research article published in the journal *Behavioral Neuroscience* found that people with a particular variation of the Catechol-*O*-methyltransferase (COMT) gene are more readily disturbed when viewing unpleasant images compared to people with a differing variation of the gene who are able to keep their emotions under control far more easily and divert them into less-obviously scare-related expressions. The urge among some people to laugh at *The Thing*'s horrific bodies might come down to genetics – maybe MacReady should have rigged up a laughter test to determine who was human and who was Thing? – or it may simply be a differently routed sociological response reflex, one that is born out of face-saving rather than biology. One of the most amusing moments in John Carpenter's and Kurt Russell's DVD feature commentary comes when Russell reacts to the Norris-Thing emergence and subsequent detached-head scuttle, particularly in response to Palmer's line 'You gotta be fucking kidding'. He can't hold in a series of full-throated laughs, peppered with 'whoa boy!', 'oh man!' 'look at that!' and other such expressions of macho delight, which in a way mimic the deadpan disbelief in Palmer's delivery. Palmer speaks for many of us; the bizarre nature of the visuals pushes the viewer to the response threshold where we are compelled to either laugh or scream in horrified disbelief.

'You gotta be fucking kidding.'

There may be even more at work here, at a still deeper subconscious level. Thinking back to Julia Kristeva's contribution to the debate about abjection and horror cinema, Eric White, in his 1993 article 'The Erotics of Becoming: XENOGENESIS and *The Thing*' published in the journal *Science Fiction Studies*, took a quote from Kristeva's 1982 'Powers of Horror' essay. In it she remarked 'the abject is edged with the sublime'. White suggested:

> The very intensity of the pleasure-pain of horror and fright may propel the viewers of this film beyond themselves, enabling them to experience, if only for a moment, the genuinely sublime prospect of no longer residing securely in their customary identities. To the extent they identify with the Thing, they would thus themselves become unclassifiable and unnameable shapeshifters. (White, 1982: 402)

For what it's worth, it has long been my experience that the extremity of the physical contortions and changes, especially on repeated viewings of the film, make it easier to regard what appears to be happening as a form of weird entertainment. Despite their human or canine form starting points and the gouts of blood that accompany the initial stages of the transformations they are ultimately alien and surreal and therefore less related to imaginable physical pain. The moments in the film that seem to genuinely unsettle those of us who might find ourselves laughing at the complex transformations are the ones involving hypodermic needles and scalpel blades puncturing the skin. These are the real 'wince moments' that can reduce a grown man, otherwise able to laugh his way through the grotesqueries of entire bodies being turned inside out, to flinching, grimacing rubble.

A scour of the many blog reviews, mostly written by young film fans not even born when *The Thing* originally came out, gives the impression that, while there is widespread acknowledgement of the film's strengths, the effects continue to split opinion. Some marvel at how well they stand up and contend that their manifest surreality and palpable, physical on-set presence compared to today's digital CGI phantoms lend the film an unnerving other-worldy quality. Others regard them as 'vintage '80s', as if that were a less than positive attribute, and run the gamut of antipathetic critical terminology from 'dubious' at one end to 'they kinda suck' at the other. Whichever side one takes the work of Rob Bottin, the conceptual illustrators and effects technicians remain a central reason why the film continues to be sought out and experienced. Just as they brought life to the assemblage of inanimate materials to achieve the ground-breaking effects so they help to breathe life into the film's reputation and reception.

'IT'S NOT DEAD YET!'

Fans have kept *The Thing* alive. After its critical burial in the permafrost of the 'thumbs-down' ice sheet and its inability to convince 1982 audiences that alien life can exist in the movies in a form other than the shuffling, heart-lit friendliness of E.T. that was worth paying money to see, *The Thing* assumed the prone position and awaited the cold pressure of the defibrillator paddles of opinion. Possibly the first goo-trickle of newly produced media, suggesting that life remained in the carcass, came in the form of Dark Horse Comics' 'The Thing from Another World' four-part miniseries which first appeared in 1991. Dark Horse specialised in reviving science fiction film franchises in graphic print form, and following their ink sequels to *Alien, Predator, The Terminator* and the like it was almost inevitable they would have their take on *The Thing*. In their 'Thing from Another World' comics, incidentally given the longer Hawks/Nyby title in order to avoid confusion and possible legal conflict with Marvel Comics' Fantastic Four member, the Thing, MacReady is the sole human survivor and Childs turns out to be infected. The comic book series would no doubt have satisfied a dedicated niche of fans at the time, eager to imagine what might have happened once the fire at the camp went out, and it contributed towards the resurrection of *The Thing* as a classic of the horror genre through its detection of a faint pulse.

When a film gets prematurely toe-tagged and consigned to the mortuary it helps the revivification process if it can gain some high profile and highly vocal supporters. Anne Billson's BFI Modern Classics book about *The Thing* featured a prominent mention of that 1990s touchstone of cool opinion Quentin Tarantino in its publicity blurb. Hot on the heels of his first two hits, *Reservoir Dogs* (1992) and *Pulp Fiction* (1994), Tarantino gave a Guardian lecture at the National Film Theatre in London on 28 January 1995 to accompany a series of film screenings at the NFT dubbed 'the Quentin Tarantino Choice season'. It was an event that attracted over 5000 ticket applications, more than ten times the seating capacity of the auditorium, so it's fair to say that the assembled audience were keen to learn which movies really mattered to the young director.

His screening choices for the season included a number of remakes, reworkings and pastiches: Godard's *À bout de souffle* (1960) but also Jim McBride's 1983 English language remake *Breathless*; De Palma's *Blow Out* (1981) which was essentially a retooling of Antonioni's *Blow Up* (1966); and a couple of Howard Hawks pictures, *His Girl Friday* and *Rio Bravo*, the latter bookended by his choice of Carpenter's *The Thing*, both 'men-under-siege' stories that resonate with *Reservoir Dogs'* all-male ensemble machismo. At the outset of his film-making career, in an interview conducted by Michel Ciment and Hubert Niogret during the 1992 Cannes Film Festival, Tarantino laid bare the debt that *Reservoir Dogs* owed to *The Thing*. It was an interview reprinted in 1998 in the book *Quentin Tarantino: Interviews* edited by Gerald Peary:

> You need to feel the claustrophobia of these guys. You need to be locked in there with them. A film that actually did that was John Carpenter's remake of *The Thing*. In some ways, it's exactly the same story as my movie. A bunch of guys are trapped in one place that they can't leave. In *The Thing* the tension and distrust and betrayal and paranoia those guys had going toward each other on that little outpost: it went right through the audience. I felt it, like a character in the movie, and it was freaking me out. That was what I was trying to achieve with *Reservoir Dogs*. I was hoping that lightning would strike twice and I could make an audience feel paranoid, creeped out, not knowing who to trust. (Peary, 1998: 16-17)

What happened to *The Thing*'s reputation in the 1990s represents a crucial stage in its journey from flop to classic. Many devotees back then, and to this day, regard it as a cult film, but does it strictly qualify? Blowing an inflated budget is one part of the standard definition, so the $15 million price tag, swollen by the eventual spend on effects, surely puts it in the cult bracket. The sum that Universal made available to Carpenter was the highest he had enjoyed up to that point, the studio figuring that he'd earned it on the back of the low budget runaway success that was Halloween (an estimated $320,000 budget) and *The Thing*'s modestly-budgeted brisk-business immediate predecessors *The Fog* and *Escape from New York* (with budgets of $1 million and $6 million respectively and US box office returns in excess $21 million and $25 million). $15 million was still high for a horror film at the time, however. For that matter it was quite high for any type of film in 1982, a year in which the average budget for a Hollywood production was around $13 million. More money was being put horror's way generally in the 1970s and 1980s thanks to box office hits like *The Exorcist* (William Friedkin, 1973) and *The Omen* (Richard Donner, 1976) and successful sci-fi/horror crossover creature features like *Alien*, which by comparison enjoyed a budget of a mere $11 million; but the bill for *The Thing* was a gamble by any stretch of the imagination. It's moderately disastrous domestic theatrical gross of less than $20 million therefore makes it a *bona fide* financial cliff-edge cult candidate.

Transgressions of taste can also help to raise a film into the realms of cultdom. Rob Bottin's approach to goriness in films is enlightening and perhaps to some surprising. In a 1982 US TV interview he countered accusations that the film was bloodthirsty by saying:

> I don't think the word is 'bloodthirsty'. As a matter of fact with *The Thing* we went out of our way to use green and yellow, magenta, a lot of bizarre colours like the rainbow instead of having people see blood. I won't work on a movie that has blood for blood's sake. I saw one movie – I'm very squeamish myself – I saw a movie called *The Deer Hunter* where they're playing Russian roulette and the blood comes out. I puked in the theatre! I can't take it. But this [*The Thing*] is imagination, this is fun, everybody knows it's not real and you're put in a situation that's fantastic, not reality. (Author's transcript)

All that being said, and assuming that audiences get that the gore is meant to be 'fun', the film's autopsy scenes alone would arguably tick the taste transgression box. Some analyses of the film recycle the story that real animal organs from a slaughterhouse were used in these scenes, which was actually not the case although it would have been if some raw meat acquired for the dissection sequence hadn't been left at the back of the Universal sound stage, gone off, stunk the place out and led to a rethink. Aside from this, dog-lovers might want to scan the end credits for reassurance that the American Humane Association oversaw the treatment of the animals. They'll find it of course, but some of those canines holed up with the Kennel-Thing were clearly capable actors when they were called upon to do 'distressed'.

Cult films are often defined by their troubled production histories. Location shooting in British Columbia certainly proved challenging; filming during the Canadian winter pushed the whole crew to its limits. There was also a hair-raising incident during a location scouting trip involving Carpenter, associate producer Larry J. Franco and co-producer Stuart Cohen in the old World War II seaplane the 'Grauman Goose'. The pilot managed to collide with another plane while he was still taxiing, damaging the Goose in the process, yet elected to take off anyway and granted his passengers a short but terrifying flight. But this was no *Apocalypse Now* (1979) or *Waterworld* (1995). Aside from the environmental demands of the location shooting and the technical and political difficulties in pulling off the special effects in time for the scheduled release, *The Thing* production personnel were a united and dedicated bunch.

Narrative ambiguities and loose ends can be prevalent cult status qualifiers. Many would say that the plot of *The Thing* has more than its fair share of blind alleys and that it is capped off with a way-too-unresolved ending. The question would be: to what extent were these narrative culs-de-sac intentional? Carpenter has stated in the past that even he was unsure exactly when the assimilated men fell victim to the organism during the process of making the film. Of course this lack of clear information imparted to the audience about the order of events only adds to the tension; it's vital to the upkeep of the suspense that we don't know for sure who at any given point is no longer human and there's much film-making wisdom at work in laying false trails.

By ticking most of the boxes then, *The Thing* can be considered a cult film on a technicality, although its rise in status as a genuine exemplar within the horror genre over the last couple of decades has been so definitive that it now seems wrong to compartmentalise it in the cult category. Champions of the film have sought to celebrate its misunderstood excellence. Indeed one of its abiding attractions is that in forwarding its dark, downbeat, nihilistic ideas it went against the grain of the shiny happy Reagan era gung ho Hollywood output of its time and over the years has come to represent a flicker of resistance that deserves to be nurtured and kindled.

The fan base that formed in the early years after the film's theatrical and home video release had to make do with a transfer to commercial tape that bore all the horrid hallmarks of 1980s products; a corner-clipping pan and scan version designed for the full screen 4:3 picture aspect ratio of the day's television sets. Even worse was the version that screened on cable TV in the US. It was extensively edited in an attempt to reduce or remove the gore, violence, drug-taking and bad language. The best that can be said about the changes is that many of the lines that got dropped into the soundtrack to disguise the profanity now rank highly in the unofficial league table of unintentionally funny over-dubs found in TV cuts from that era. Here's a selection:

'...weird and *ticked off* whatever it is.'

'...you buy any of this voodoo bull*stuff*?'

'...how's this *monkeyfellow* wake up?'

'...hey, *fry* you Palmer!'

'...tied to this *stinking* couch!'

'...yeah, *blast* you too!'

The cable cut also had an opening sequence narration added to introduce the film's characters, an entirely unnecessary voice-over laid onto the scene in which Blair uses his computer to calculate the organism's rate of global infection and an extraneous alternative ending.[14] Matters improved significantly in the 1990s. That cumbersome foundation stone of DVD technology, the Laserdisc, was clinging on to its bit of the home video entertainment market; after a mid-1980s disc release of the pan and scan version in the U.S. around the same time as the videotape edition a properly letterboxed version of *The Thing* made its first appearance in the American market in 1990. This disc bore only a few extras but in 1994 Universal Studio Home Video announced a new series of Laserdisc releases, the Signature Collection, which characteristically boasted bags of bonus features; supplemental materials, theatrical trailers, promotional materials, exclusive documentaries with video interviews, storyboards, screen tests, scripts, behind-the-scenes footage and running commentaries. As the title of the series suggests, each disc sleeve carried the signature of the film's director. The Carpenter quote on the reverse side of the sleeve reads: 'THE THING truly has the same quality on Laserdisc that the movie did.'

It was around the time of the start-up of the Signature Collection that documentary director Michael Matessino was approached by Universal with a view to contributing to the special features on future releases. The result was the 83-minute film *The Thing: Terror Takes Shape*. According to Matessino himself:

They offered me *The Thing*. I set about contacting all the film-makers and began scheduling interviews and it went on from there with the studio's tremendous support. The first discussions were in 1995, so at first I was surprised they wanted to do it, but I was starting to become aware that there were a lot of movies that didn't do well theatrically which played over and over on cable during the 1980s, and that the younger movie fans of that era were the ones who were investing in Laserdisc and who were interested in special features. They were also the early adopters for DVD. The project was stalled when DVD started getting talked about and the release was held back so that it would come out on both formats. Certainly by that time I was well aware of the fan base and how excited they were about it. (Author's interview)

The Laserdisc release of *The Thing* on 8 September 1998 coincided with the film's first release on DVD. This was an early entry in Universal's Collector's Edition DVD series and carried exactly the same extras as the Laserdisc, including Matessino's documentary, which has proved to be one of the most enduring features on pretty much every subsequent iteration of the film, right up to and including the 2008 Blu-ray release. What *Terror Takes Shape* lacks in fine analytical detail it more than makes up for in capturing the essence of what it was like to make the film from the perspective of the major players. Michael Matessino again:

I was thrilled by the stories that were recounted and by how much cast and crew loved working on it, and that camaraderie is what I tried to capture in the show while still maintaining the mood of the film itself. I think that the fans responded to that. It's very easy to just document *how* a movie is made, but I like to always try to give the viewer a sense of *who* the people are and to explore how the dynamic of that particular group combined to create the film that got made. (Author's interview)

By the late 1990s the global interconnectivity of the World Wide Web had initiated a huge push way beyond the long-established fan culture boundaries of conventions and fanzines and had rapidly lead to the coalescence of mass online fan communities with a shared, ardent, often obsessive adoration for particular films. The outsider protagonists of Carpenter's films were made to be loved by these sub-cultural internet fan communities. *The Thing* in particular generated a considerable number of fan-made websites, frequently equipped with forums and discussion boards in which devotees could discuss the finer points of the film for as long as their 56K dial-up internet connection would allow.

The mother of all *Thing* fansites, Outpost#31, went online in October 2001. It was co-founded by Todd Cameron and Chris Morgan with major contributions from the now sadly deceased Steve Crawford and a legion of long term loyal followers. The site's creators have done much to convene collective opinion and enthusiasm for the film; in among the treasury of tidbits, trivia, original articles, fan fiction and just about anything and everything you might wish to know about the film you will find a growing number of Q&As with cast and crew members. Between 2001 and 2008 the site's creators organised THING-FEST, an annual get-together for fans complete with a screening of the film. THING-FEST was reconvened in 2012 to mark the thirtieth anniversary of the film. The website also tells of Todd and Steve's sojourn to Stewart, British Columbia in 2003 in search of the exact spot where location filming of the research station took place. There they found remnants of the exploded Norwegian helicopter and took back a treasured memento – one of the rotor blades complete with scorch marks from the explosion. The website's influence can be measured in a quote retrospectively added to the 2008 memorial page for the late Crawford from Matthijs van Heijningen Jr., director of the 2011 *Thing* prequel:

> When I started to explore the Norwegian story, fantasizing what could have happened there, I needed to know the exact layout of the base and I quickly landed at outpost31.com. I was really thrilled to discover all the maps of Outpost #31 and the Norwegian base. I printed them out, put them in my office and studied them. I compared them with the JC footage and realized that they were accurate. That is how it all started. Thanks to Steve Crawford. (van Heijningen Jr./Outpost#31 2011/2008)

Special annual screenings haven't been limited to THING-FESTs. As previously mentioned, every February, on the evening of the day that marks the last flight out of the Antarctic continent before the overwinter period commences, the hardy few destined to remain at Amundsen-Scott South Pole Station for the duration are treated to a showing of the film, usually in a double feature with *The Shining*, presumably just in case watching *The Thing* on its own isn't enough to scare the pants off a group of people about to spend the next few months of wintry isolation in close proximity to each other.

Over the last decade, thanks in large part to the rise of video sharing websites, the number of web-based homages, parodies and skits based on *The Thing* has grown and grown. A modern sign of successful notoriety or the attainment of the status of 'classic' comes when a film gets the *South Park* treatment. Sure enough, the episode *Lice Capades*, which first aired on Comedy Central in the States on 21 March 2007 contains a major reference to the blood test sequence; Cartman uses a hot needle to test blood samples as a way to find out who's infested. A casual search of YouTube will quickly find several tongue-in-cheek recreations. There's a claymation version that mixes *The Thing* with the plasticine penguin character Pingu and sees the film's main effects sequences recreated amid the igloos. There's a computer-generated animation, put together by the people at PeepholeCircus, set rather bizarrely in the studio of Channel Four's afternoon quiz show *Countdown* which ends bloodily. There's a musical skit made by brothers Jon and Al Caplan using clips from the film overlaid with a Sinatra sound-a-like singing his way through the film's plot in the swing style. And there's more than one charmingly ultra low-tech 'sweded' version put together by the requisite band of recklessly dedicated and presumably near-penniless fanboys. There has even been a live action stage version of the film; a small theatre in San Francisco recently mounted a play based on *The Thing* that attempted to recreate the key effects sequences in real time before the very eyes of its audience.

Claycat's THE THING

Lee Hardcastle, the maker of the Pingu animated version, whose work has progressed to inclusion in full blown cinematic horror anthology *The ABCs of Death* (26 directors, 2012) alongside the likes of *Kill List*'s (2011) Ben Wheatley , was honest and open about his affection for *The Thing* when asked:

Me and *The Thing* go way back. I first saw it on television when I was eight and I actually missed the first part of the movie so I saw all the horrible parts in the second half which scared the hell out of me. I was keen to know the back story so I bought it on VHS (which was the first I ever bought) – I remember for a whole week once, every night after school I'd pop it in the VCR. I fell in love with it. It's been close to my heart ever since and I've watched it a hundred times, it never gets old. (Author's interview)

In mentioning Wheatley, the new kid on the British crime/horror crossover block, it's worth noting that *The Thing* is also one of his favourite films. Invited to compile his top ten horrific films for the Film4 website he placed *The Thing* at number seven saying:

I am a massive Carpenter fan. I watch *The Thing* a couple of times a year. The creature effects still stand up and are revolting. Rob Bottin's eye for detail is incredible: The dog spitting the weird liquid over the other dogs, the wriggly tendrils shaking around out of the heart attack victim's chest, the spider head! (Wheatley, 2013)

A contemporary of Wheatley's, the young British writer-director Sean Hogan, who feature-debuted with the low rent critical hit *The Devil's Business* in 2012, was sufficiently inspired by *The Thing*'s blood test sequence to riff on it in his 2011 short *The Thing: 27,000 Hours*. In a twist, the character wielding the hot needle is delighted when the blood leaps from the Petri dish. It signals which one of the two tethered men whose blood he's testing is, just like himself, a Thing.

The influence of *The Thing* has crossed over into other areas of the arts. Contemporary visual artists Christine Sullivan and Rob Flint's 2011 performative work 'The Thing Is' involved the artists sitting in a synthetically cocooned gallery space wearing video glasses and simultaneously viewing the two film versions, one watching 1951's *The Thing from Another World*, the other watching the 1982 Carpenter film. The performance involved Sullivan and Flint describing their experience as it took place. Watching the films for the first time, each described their specific movie in parallel at opposite ends of the space, while the audience moved freely between them, assembling a second-hand narrative from re-told stories separated by three decades.

Ronnie van Hout, a New Zealand artist living in Melbourne, has a long-standing relationship with *The Thing*. His work, which encompasses sculpture, video, painting, photography, embroidery, and sound recordings, has drawn on imagery and ideas from the film on more than one occasion. Indeed his life seems inextricably linked to the film. Van Hout himself explains:

It started in late 1982. I was about to finish my studies at art school when I was encouraged by some older students to apply for a job as a kitchen hand to winter over at Scott Base [not to be confused with the previously mentioned American research base Amundsen-Scott South Pole Station] in Antarctica. The evening before my interview for the job I went to a screening of John Carpenter's *The Thing*. The film's imagery did its work on my subconscious and contributed on some level to my fluffing the interview. However in 2006 a friend suggested I apply to be an artist-in-residence at Scott Base. My application used John W. Campbell's source novella 'Who Goes There?' and other fictional accounts of Antarctica as reference points for exploration and the creation of new work. The themes of replication, abjection and aliens that are so present in *The Thing* have probably been some of the main concerns of my art practise. A requirement of the Antarctic residency was to make an artwork based on my experiences. My first attempt was to make a sculptural work to be shown as a part of a mini-survey exhibition of my work at the Christchurch Art Gallery, New Zealand in 2009. The title of the survey was 'Who Goes There?' Making casts of objects is a large part of my practice, and come out of an interest in the copy and its role and relationship to the original. Non-sexual reproduction, or pathogenesis, is a strong theme throughout *The Thing*. I made a fibreglass copy of myself wearing my Antarctic cold weather gear, sitting in a white room. The room was dark until someone pressed a large red button to turn on the lights. The figure in this work titled '*The Thing*' sits impassively, a trickle of blood from its nose, an indication that maybe it is infected. (Author's interview)

Not satisfied with confining his Thing-influenced work to this installation, van Hout returned to the source more recently:

In 2011, I wanted to make a number of short videos around the idea of acting, with its implications of playing a role, inhabiting and becoming another. Campbell wrote 'Who Goes There?' as a response to his conflicted feelings toward his mother. The story goes that Campbell's mother had an identical twin sister that he could not distinguish from his real mother. His mother's sister would reject the young Campbell's attempts to gain physical comfort, and he instead gained a feeling that people, even close ones, could not be trusted. The video work I made was titled 'The Other Mother', and is a copy of the blood testing scene from *The Thing*. Typically, I play all the parts, shot and edited this work. I think the blood-testing scene is one of the most pivotal in *The Thing*, and even though the film contains many scenes of abject horror, this one wreaks havoc. It is the scene that makes a mess, where things are broken as chaos ensues. It is the infantile pant-shitting scene, the 'take that, mother!' scene. (Author's interview)

The 2000s saw a fresh interactivity emerge in *Thing*-related spin-offs. In 2002 a third person survival horror shoot 'em up game version for Play Station and Xbox appeared. Developed by Computer Artworks and published under the Black Label Games banner, a collaboration between Universal Interactive and Konami, *The Thing* video game had a plot set a few days after the events of the Carpenter film and came as close to canonical as a game ever could, gaining help in that respect from an uncredited vocal character performance by John Carpenter as Dr. Sean Faraday. *The Thing 2* game was shelved when Computer Artworks ceased business in 2004 but it's thought that some of the monster designs that were developed inspired the creatures that would eventually be seen in the 2011 prequel film. In 2007 Universal Studios in Orlando, Florida unveiled *The Thing: Assimilation*, a *Thing*-themed walk-through 'creature maze' attraction as part of its Halloween Horror Nights event. Another sequel of sorts, visitors were treated to the sight of MacReady and Childs stored in cryogenic chambers and animatronic recreations of various Thing manifestations. Similar attractions appeared in 2011 at both Universal theme parks in Florida and Hollywood to mark the release of the prequel.

Years before the 2011 prequel drilled down to explore the pre-Carpenter period, other film-makers and television creatives were extracting core samples from *The Thing*'s substrate and incorporating elements into their work. The eighth episode of the first season of *The X Files*, screened in November 1993 and entitled 'Ice', drew on the

Campbell novella for inspiration and borrowed heavily from the Carpenter film for its visuals. 'Ice' had more in common with *The Thing* than first meets the eye; its production designer was Graeme Murray who twelve years earlier had worked as set decorator during the Stewart location shooting on the Carpenter film. More recently director Larry Fessenden's *The Last Winter* (2006) successfully borrowed *The Thing*'s cold-sweat claustrophobic paranoia and applied it to its Arctic-set eco-horror plot concerning the effects on the crew at an oil company's drilling station of escaped poison gas. Mark A. Lewis's *The Thaw* (2009) dipped its rod into a very similar ice hole with its story of a prehistoric parasite freed from a melting Arctic ice cap thanks to global warming. By dropping a planeload of oil workers in the Alaskan wastes and pitting them against a pack of ravenous wolves, Joe Carnahan's *The Grey* (2011) defrosted a hybrid of Jack London, *The Thing* and Frank Marshall's *Alive* (1993) for its entirely terrestrial terrors.

One recent film has reached the parts that even John Carpenter couldn't get to. *South of Sanity*, a British horror film released on Halloween night 2012 was shot entirely in Antarctica, the first feature length film able to boast this claim, and almost inevitably doffed its parka hood in the direction of *The Thing*. It's a low-budget tale of bloody murder amid snowy isolation with a cast of characters who are kept guessing as to the identity of the killer. *South of Sanity*'s producer/director/writer/actor team of Kirk Watson and Mathew Edwards were able to draw upon their own experiences of living at the bottom of the world when making the film and can confirm that *The Thing* is a favourite of yet more Antarctic bases. Watson explains:

> It has been traditional on British Antarctic Survey bases to watch *The Thing* on mid-winters day every year since 1982. At Rothera Research Station there are probably 12–15 copies of it on the shelf in the library. Every year a new recruit brings a copy in thinking it should be watched. I have watched it three times on three separate mid-winters days. Our film is set at Rothera Research Station so recently we have been played alongside *The Thing* which Matt and myself see as the greatest honour our film could have. (Author's interview)

South of Sanity (Mathew Edwards, Kirk Watson 2012)

The appearance of the Matthijs van Heijningen Jr. prequel in 2011, although in some senses a culmination of fan-fuelled interest in a further exploration of the ideas contained within the Carpenter film, was a reasonably predictable release given the prevailing trend of originality-deficient reboots and remakes that has characterised studio horror cinema in recent years. There is now a big body of evidence to show that one of the many after-effects of 9/11 was the pressing of a horror genre reset button, after which dispassionate cold-blooded torture and cruel butchery at the hands of sadistic outsiders became the dominant meme for onscreen terror. This can be seen in the influential abattoir austerity of the *Saw* (2004 onwards) and *Hostel* (2005 onwards) films, which have successfully if cynically refreshed audience fears for their safety, films with a look and feel that has bled, if you will, into countless subsequent horror releases. Their success has prompted producers and studios to blow the dust off many of their horror properties and represent them for a new generation of viewers raised to expect their fright experiences swathed in a blood-stained executioner's apron. Although the *Thing* prequel's horror/science fiction crossover sits less comfortably with the prevalent chopping board realism there is something in the perennial who's who paranoia found in van Heijningen Jr.'s film, and unquestionably also in Carpenter's film, which well reflects the last decade's post-9/11 mood of mistrust. The current Outpost#31 webmaster, 'Tony' aka 'Xidioux' had this say on the matter:

> When someone 'Things out', as we like to say, it's like a suicide bomber, doing what they do, in slow-motion: destroying themselves and taking others down with them.

You can go further with this correspondence: assimilation = indoctrination, etc... As long as there is a reason to fear the 'other', *The Thing* will be relevant and applicable. (Author's interview)

This reboot tendency has also been driven by technical advances; modern CGI effects can now more graphically render the signature carnage and digital high definition along with new 3D screening technology allowing film-makers the opportunity to project their gore right into the viewer's lap. The simple nostalgic affection for the now-classic scare-fests of the 1970s and 1980s, whose time has come to be passed from one generation of viewers to the next, cannot be discounted as another explanation for the appearance of so many franchise restarts. Mostly however the trend has been steered by the financial expediency of recycling 'known quantity' brands, especially those for which the remake rights paperwork already resided safely in film studio vaults. There are few hit horrors from those earlier decades that *haven't* received the reboot treatment at some point since the turn of the millennium, and it must be said that very few have managed to bring any fresh meat to the table. If anything they have risked inflicting a reductive effect on the collective audience memory of the original films that inspired them.

The van Heijningen Jr. prequel met with critical ambivalence, fan uncertainty and unspectacular, fair-to-middling box office returns upon its release. Ironically, by garnering this relatively equivocal reaction and avoiding the near-blanket negativity that the Carpenter film received back in 1982 it has increased its chances of being forgotten – for the record I shall happily eat my words when somebody writes a book about its gradual rise in reputation thirty years from now – but unlike other recent horror brand restoratives it cannot really be said to have done a major disservice to the reputation of its antecedent. Damning with faint praise perhaps, but nevertheless true. While it may have lapsed into routine plotting, lacked recognisable diversity among its characters and fallen back on a scenario of sexual tension and the near-inevitable Final Girl resolution, it took great pains to set up the events of Carpenter's film, so much so that the two films could conceivably be spliced together for a continual viewing experience. This is testament to a confident, perhaps naive, belief that such seamlessness would matter to today's audiences. Also to van Heijningen Jr.'s credit is his desire to stick with practical rather than digital effects for his Thing creations. In the end what made it to the screen was a hybrid of on-set animatronic puppetry and computer-generated effects, a combination that still lacks the solidity of Rob Bottin's efforts, but is nonetheless a brave attempt to recapture the viscerality of its predecessor.

It remains to be seen if the prequel's commercial underperformance means that the *Thing* franchise, if indeed it is a franchise, is interred once again in cold storage. Van Heijningen Jr.'s film, for all of its shortcomings, may well have brought a new young audience to the Carpenter film who, just like those before them, will have to deal with its downbeat, ambiguous resolution. There are certainly no signs of a further film to resolve MacReady's story and complete a protracted trilogy, so in all likelihood the fans, old and new, will have to continue to ponder just what happens to the helicopter pilot once the fires at Outpost 31 have finally died out. Which brings us on to *that* ending…

'WHY DON'T WE JUST...WAIT HERE FOR A LITTLE WHILE...SEE WHAT HAPPENS...'

Endings don't come much more downbeat than the final moments of *The Thing*. The best that the two surviving humans (if we presume them both to be human at that point) can hope for is a rapid death numbed by whisky and hypothermia and the satisfaction that through their demise they have denied the Thing access to living tissue and the prospect of reaching the rest of humanity. For MacReady at least it's an act of bleakly heroic suicide.

The Thing came along during a period when a film's sequel potential was a likely contributory factor in it getting the green light. The 1980s and 1990s were littered with cookie-cutter cash cow sequels; there were more *Police Acadamies*, *Poltergeists*, *Psychos* and *Porkys* than you could snap a clapperboard at. For every two *Crocodile Dundees* (1986, 1988) there were three *Beverley Hills Cops* (1984, 1987, 1994); for every three *Look Who's Talkings* (1989, 1990, 1993) there were four *Karate Kids* (1984, 1986, 1989, 1994). *The Thing*'s necessarily terrible finality was, short of a risible leap of plausibility in any attempted follow-on film, tantamount to sequel suicide.

Looking at a wider span of time it's possible to discern a historical pattern of happy/ unhappy Hollywood endings down the decades, denouements that not only reflect their times but actually help to portray the upbeat tide of the 1980s, against which *The Thing* swam, as less frequently favoured than one might perhaps imagine. The last reels of the film noir movies of the 1940s and 1950s tended towards the pessimistic, and the 1960s and 1970s were strewn with melancholic finales. John Hartl's Seattle Times article 'Is There An End In Sight For The Happy-Ending Trend?' published in 1992, perhaps not entirely coincidentally around the time of *The Thing*'s first proper reappraisal, helped to chart this pattern. Of the pre-Reagan era he wrote:

> The world blew up in *Dr. Strangelove*. Bonnie and Clyde and The Wild Bunch were massacred. *McCabe and Mrs. Miller* ended with the hero bleeding to death in the snow. Dustin Hoffman didn't survive to see the promised land of Florida in *Midnight Cowboy*. Jack Nicholson underwent a lobotomy in *One Flew Over the Cuckoo's Nest*.

Ali MacGraw played a young wife who died in the hugely successful *Love Story*. (Hartl, 1993)

The Thing had its tentacles planted firmly in this tradition. 1970s Hollywood in particular reflected the post-Vietnam, post-Watergate national malaise through its string of disaster films in which even the most heroic deeds had to exist in the context of almost inevitable mass destruction. Anyone still drawing breath at the end of *The Poseidon Adventure* (Ronald Neame, 1972), *The Towering Inferno* (John Guillermin, 1974), *Earthquake* (Mark Robson, 1974) and any of the four *Airport* films (1970–1979) usually had basic survival as their only reward.

The temporary shift towards the sunlit uplands of 1980s optimism began with the blockbusters of the mid-to-late 1970s. *Rocky* (John G. Avildsen, 1976) punched the air and lived to fight another day (five other days and still counting) and if anyone important died in *Star Wars* (George Lucas, 1977) they simply came back as a wise and possibly eternal spiritual entity in the sequels. By the time of the early 1990s, with a political shift away from three terms of Republicanism in the US, the informed postmodern cynicism of Robert Altman's *The Player* (1992) was closer to the prevailing mood. With its eventual ludicrous film-within-a film conclusion featuring a heroic Bruce Willis rescuing a wrongly-convicted Julia Roberts from the gas chamber seconds before execution, here was a film that pointedly spoofed the impossibly happy endings of the previous decade. For a while the sombre, downbeat ending was tolerated and even regarded as bankable, typified by the moral ambiguities and dark sentiments of *Unforgiven* (Clint Eastwood, 1992) and the closing moments of *Se7en* (David Fincher, 1995), a film in which the central character Detective Lt. Somerset (Morgan Freeman) telegraphs the tragic conclusion half an hour before the end credits roll with his line 'This isn't going to have a happy ending'. It's a line that echoes the foresight of Palmer's early declaration in *The Thing*: 'I know how this one ends.'

By the end of the 1990s screen apocalypses in the late-Clinton, pre-millennial period tended towards the fantastical and ultimately victorious. Potential extraterrestrial end-of-the-world scenarios in films such as *Independence Day* (Roland Emmerich, 1996), *Deep Impact* (Mimi Leder, 1998) and *Armageddon* (Michael Bay, 1998) were frequently resolved through acts of patriotic machismo and limited self-sacrifice which led to the life-affirming macro/micro restoration of divided communities and broken relationships. In the wake of 9/11 these films seemed to possess a consequence-free naivety. It took some time for Hollywood to look destruction in the face again after the 2001 attacks on the World Trade Center, but when it did it was an overriding sense of panicked unpreparedness in the face of barely visible enemies or circumstances that became the basis for response to global threats. Look at the chaos and loss experienced by the characters amid the mist, dust and ash in *The Mist* (Frank Darabont, 2007), *Cloverfield* (Matt Reeves, 2008) and *The Road* (John Hillcoat, 2009); ordinary people thrown into turmoil by unexpected events, running away from or stumbling into oblivion to face an indiscriminate fate that spares them little or no pity. The occluding and enveloping death-white fog and smoke captured in these films drew heavily on the ashen clouds of destruction that all Americans saw on their television screens in 2001. There's a resonance to these clouds of disarray to be found in *The Thing*'s obliterating blanket of snow, isolating conditions that pay no respect to human social order and rob people of their identity.

A nice nod to the importance *The Thing* now plays in the new pessimism of these post-9/11 films can be spotted in the first few moments of Darabont's *The Mist*. Main character David Drayton (Thomas Jane) is a professional film poster artist and the opening shot of the film shows him at work in his studio with examples of his previous work displayed on the walls. The posters used were the handiwork of the artist Drew Struzan whose illustrative talents provided the poster art for the *Indiana Jones*, *Star Wars*, *Back to the Future* and *Rambo* films, among many others. By far the most visible poster on Drayton's wall is Struzan's now-famous painting used for *The Thing*'s original publicity material. In this context the brilliant white light emerging from the parka hood could almost be a beacon to Drayton warning him of the monstrously extra-terrestrial events that are about to unfold in his life. It also drops a hint to the audience that *The Mist* itself would end on a devastating low, which of course it did, quite likely a contributory cause to its set of disappointing box office statistics (US domestic total gross of $25,594, 957 with an $18 million production budget) which closely mirrors *The Thing*'s original theatrical performance.

The Mist (Frank Darabont 2007)

In mentioning Darabont it's worth adding that his link to *The Thing* goes deeper than poaching its poster for set decoration. In 2005 the Sci-Fi Channel announced that it would make a *Thing* sequel with Darabont serving as a producer. This project was to be a four-hour mini-series written by Darabont's former assistant David Leslie Johnson and broadcast on the cable channel. This never came to fruition but represents the first steps Universal took along the path towards rekindling its property which eventually resulted in the van Heijningen Jr. prequel.

It's perhaps not widely known that Carpenter shot three different endings for *The Thing*: the one that was eventually used, one in which Childs disappears into the snowy night leaving MacReady alone and one showing MacReady awaiting a final blood test at McMurdo Station. This third alternative is the closest the director came to providing closure, and one that co-producer Stuart Cohen has confirmed was never seriously intended to be used. The way the film was going to end became a bone of contention as production entered its final phase and concern about test audience response to the favoured ending arose. Cohen explains further:

> As production on the film proceeded a number of important voices raised concerns that the film was becoming too dark and depressing, and that we should think about a 'happier' or more 'finite' conclusion. We held an early screening of the unfinished film sometime in late March 1981 for invited friends and family. John fielded questions and asked for reaction afterwards and a fair number of them raised questions about it as well.

Matters reached critical mass at the first preview in Las Vegas, the first time both a paying audience and Universal's executives would see the film. Reaction was not good from either quarter, with many preview cards angrily speaking about the ending. I think now that we underestimated the cumulative power of this film on a large screen sprung on an unsuspecting audience for the first time and by the time we reached the final confrontation with the two men it simply exhausted and depressed a fair number of them. We were asked to take a look at the ending again to see if we could wrap up the film on a more positive note.

After a week in which suggestions were offered and tried from many quarters a new version of the film was previewed on Friday night to an invited audience on the Universal lot, one in which Childs simply disappears completely off-screen earlier in the film, much like both Fuchs and Nauls, leaving MacReady alone at the end to battle the monster and freeze to death. This new version was previewed alongside the original in an adjoining screening room, the audiences' reaction then compared. There was a very slight uptick in approval for the new version, maybe three per cent. Armed with this information the chorus of voices looking for a finite conclusion briefly prevailed, and John and the rest of us acceded to their wishes and signed off on the new version.

I felt terrible about this the next morning; [it] turned out so did John and everyone else, and on Monday we organised a meeting with Universal's President to plead our case to restore things the way they were. I stated that I would rather leave the audience with a question than with nothing at all, and additionally the preview cards demonstrated that the audience really didn't much care for either ending, so why not do the right thing dramatically for the movie? Universal did the responsible thing and allowed us to put the original ending back, one day before final release printing was to begin. (Author's interview)

From this then we know that the ending that we finally got was the ending most favoured by Carpenter himself. But while respect is due for persisting with a completion to the story that knowingly risked alienating audiences, many still find it hard to defend the film's considerable number of loose ends. Many questions arise during the film that fail to find definite answers by the end; what follows is an inexhaustive selection:

- Who exactly does the Norwegian dog assimilate? We see the profile shadow of a man on the wall turn to look at the dog as it enters the room but we never do know for sure which of the men at Outpost 31 it's about to leap on.

- A part of the Kennel-Thing appears to break through the ceiling timbers midway through the assimilation process and raise itself up and out through the roof. What happens to it after that?

- When MacReady, Norris and Palmer visit the crashed saucer site what's stopping them from taking a look inside the craft? The hatch is clearly open. Perhaps, given that in all likelihood both Norris and Palmer are both already assimilated Thing copies they worked together to dissuade MacReady from doing that, although this begs another question: Why didn't these two Things assimilate MacReady at the saucer site when they had the chance?

- Who tampered with the refrigerated blood supply in order to scupper Copper's chances of conducting his test? We might later think that it must be one of either Blair, Norris or Palmer but we don't know for sure.

- What were the circumstances of Fuchs' death? MacReady suspects suicide; maybe so, but however he came to die the passage of time in which he burns to death and is reduced to cinders, rendered recognisable only when his spectacles are discovered in the pile of charred and completely extinguished remains, is remarkably short.

- How and when does Nauls die or become assimilated? We never do see what happens to him towards the end and the best we can assume is that he is assimilated by Blair around the time that Garry is attacked, and therefore along with Garry (again assuming) he forms a subsumed part of the greater Blair-Thing that rears up before MacReady.

- When is Blair assimilated? Knowing this would shed a totally different light on his actions throughout the film. It could be as early as his autopsy of the Split-Face Thing – the viscera that he extracts in the procedure could have got to him off-camera – or it could be as late as during his incarceration in the tool shed. The most likely answer is somewhere in between but we have no way to be sure.

I could go on, but the risk is that this would seem like a big list of criticisms, suggesting that Carpenter strayed into basic continuity errors and simple plot oversights. Perhaps he did make mistakes, but in light of this book's examination of why *The Thing* works so well, I would ask: do any of these questions actually matter? I would even go as far as to suggest that the numerous dead ends, red herrings, false trails and missing explanations, added to that famously unresolved ending, are one of the main reasons why the film works as well as it does. Carpenter's overarching aim was disruption; he sought to pull recognisable reality inside out in so many ways so it should not be surprising that he also sought to disrupt the narrative. Without all of these unanswered questions cropping up during the film viewers would be less decentred, so plot uncertainty is an integral part of the *Thing* effect.

Having said all that, there is a surprising number of quite neat top-and-tail 'bookend' moments to be found in the film if one were to focus on the early sightings and eventual fates of many of the characters and apply a little creative interpretation. Again how much of this was intentional on the part of the film-makers is open to debate, but if nothing else it's entertaining to consider each character's story as a capsule with a beginning and an end denoted by their onscreen actions. For example:

- Blair: early on we see him hacking into the Kennel-Thing remains to reveal dog copies and at the end the assimilated Blair-Thing is sprouting dog copies of his own from its pulsating abdomen.

- Garry: his reaction to the sight of the Split-Face Thing is to put his hand over his mouth to hold back vomit, but it's Blair's hand smothering his mouth when the station manager gets assimilated.

- Copper: the first time we see the surgeon's hands at work they are suturing Bennings' gunshot wound ('C'mon, four stitches, barely grazed you') – the last time they're being chewed up by the Norris-Thing's stomach maw.

- Windows: we see him firstly with his head clasped between the two soft pads of his large headphones trying to reach radio contact and lastly with it crushed between the two tusked mandibles of the Palmer-Thing's head maw.

- Bennings: there he is on his knees in the snow having been shot in the leg by the Norwegian and there he is again, in Bennings-Thing form, on his knees in the snow about to be set alight for falling short of completing assimilation.

- Fuchs: he's one of the men staring at the charred remains of the Norwegian helicopter pilot at the beginning and after his death his own similarly incinerated remnants are stood over and stared at.

- Norris: he's at the head-end of the Split-Face Thing when it's revealed to the men, stood looking down at this monstrosity, and he'll be laid on the same operating table being looked down on by the other men later when he gets to do his Thing.

And what of MacReady? As discussed earlier, our first glimpse of him is in close-up drinking his J&B and our last is much the same. In the interim his world has turned itself upside down and inside out, but by presenting him swigging his drink of choice at both beginning and end there is a reinforcement of sorts that he is the same man (i.e. human) at the end as he was at the beginning.

Possibly the biggest question that fans have been trying to find an answer to in the intervening years concerns the humanity, or otherwise, of both MacReady and Childs as they slump in front of the flaming guts of Outpost 31. There will probably always be a school of thought that will insist MacReady was assimilated at some earlier stage. A MacReady-Thing, knowing that it must make do with a stalemate result in the Outpost 31 scenario, would arguably seek to kill all the remaining humans and wait to freeze in the snow so that it can be discovered by a fresh batch of rescuing humans at some point in the future. Another lobby of opinion will tell you that MacReady is indeed still human and that Childs is a Thing; between disappearing in the snow having thought he saw Blair and reappearing before MacReady his jacket appears to have changed, suggesting that his original clothes have been ripped due to assimilation and this Childs-Thing needed a quick wardrobe change. Besides, if you look closely at the final scene you can't see breath vapour emerging from his mouth in the same way that MacReady's is visible, which surely mark him out as no longer human, doesn't it? Actually if you look closely and borrow the principle illustrated in the 2011 prequel that Things can't assimilate metal objects, the fact that Childs' earring is still visible in the final scenes would suggest that

'Fire's got the temperature up all over the camp. Won't last long though.'

he's human after all. A third position will put forward the notion that by the end both men are Things; they are waiting there for a little while to see what happens and toasting their victory.

My favourite piece of conjecture once again links MacReady's opening scene with his last. When he loses to the Chess Wizard computer he gets his own back by pouring some of his precious J&B into its insides causing the machine to spark and die. Could it be that by passing Childs the bottle of whisky to drink from he knows that the man before him is no longer a man and that he's pouring more J&B into his final assailant before destroying him? Perhaps, though, the actual solution is the bleakest of all; that both MacReady *and* Childs are both still human and that they will duly die together as humans.

The final answer to this final question is of course: all or none of the above. The point is to ponder all of the possibilities. Therein lies *The Thing's* bleak and frightening entertainment. Now pass me that bottle of J&B.

NOTES

1. The American Antarctic research station is now routinely referred to in *Thing* lore as Outpost 31, despite the fact that during our first sight of it in the film there is a large sign outside the main building which clearly reads 'United States National Science Institute Station 4'. By the second draft script stage screenwriter Bill Lancaster was calling the base Outpost 31 and in the film MacReady signs off an audio diary tape recording 'R.J. MacReady, helicopter pilot, U.S. Outpost 31'. In attempting to reach McMurdo Station on his radio equipment Windows also refers to the base as 'US Number 31'. The name stuck and you will struggle to find any conflicting reference to the base by any other name. Some think, with good reason, that the name arose originally as a nod to Carpenter's earlier hit *Halloween* thanks to the similarity to the 31st October date of that film's setting.

2. Although every formal source will tell you that *The Thing from Another World* was directed by Christian Nyby, anyone in the know, including John Carpenter, regards it as a Howard Hawks picture through and through. Nyby had been Hawks' editor on *To Have And Have Not*, *The Big Sleep*, *Red River* and *The Big Sky*, and had performed similar duties throughout the 1940s for directors such as Raoul Walsh, Delmer Daves and Fritz Lang. The thinking is that Hawks allowed Nyby to take the director credit so that he could gain membership of the Directors Guild of America. Nyby's subsequent directing work, mostly in television for shows like *Perry Mason*, *Bonanza* and *The Six Million Dollar Man*, doesn't exactly replicate the command of the medium on display in *The Thing from Another World*, which, despite Hawks' own assertion to the contrary, rather betrays the fact that it was he who called the shots on the film.

3. In an interview with George Hickenlooper that featured in the 1991 book 'Reel Conversations: Candid Interviews With Film's Foremost Directors and Critics', Carpenter referred to his conscious attempts to avoid following received wisdom which would have him hide the Thing out of plain sight:

    > I knew I either had to show the monster or not show it, but put it in shadows. All the literary critics and all the left-wing folks think, well, you shouldn't show the monster because that's kind of tacky and poo-poo. Well, there's another way of going about it. And, boy, if you do it right, if you hit a home run, you create the greatest monster of all time... So that's what we did. We decided to put it under the lights and create a monster like no other seen before. (Carpenter, 1991: 337)

4. This key-drop is actually a significant clue to a plot question that many viewers miss; when the base's blood supply is tampered with the main conflict arises over who had access to the bunch of master keys that included the one that opened the freezer containing the blood. In

the heat of the argument everyone forgets that Windows had the keys last when putting the Split-Face Thing into the storage room. After he dropped the keys and ran off upon witnessing the Bennings-Thing we can reasonably assume that a Thing, probably Blair, picked them up and took the opportunity to damage the blood.

5.   The gutted remains of the Norwegian base are in fact the same buildings that were used for Outpost 31. The exterior scenes with MacReady and Copper discovering the Split-Face Thing in the snow outside the Norwegian base were shot after the Outpost 31 buildings were torched for the film's finale. Incidentally the Norwegian helicopter that gets blown up at the beginning of the film and the helicopter that MacReady flies are also one and the same.

6.   'As You Know, Bob', sometimes abbreviated to AYKB, is the term that has come to describe a character in film or fiction whose function it is to deliver plot exposition through their dialogue. These custodians of the info dump were especially rife in post-war science fiction, where they were often required to articulate weighty scientific technobabble as best they could for the edification of mere mortals. It would then fall upon a 'Tell Me, Professor' character, such as Scotty in *The Thing from Another World* to make sense of the science on behalf of Joe Public sitting in row K. This they would do typically with a tilt of their hat to the crown of their head and a four-fingernail scratch of their fevered brow. The 'Tell Me, Professor' and 'As You Know, Bob' roles in the Carpenter film aren't quite so clearly defined; on balance it's Childs who's handed the most 'let me get this straight, Doc' type lines, while Blair, being the nearest equivalent to Carrington, is the AYKB by default.

7.   Operation Eagle Claw was the name given to the failed American military operation that sought to rescue the 53 hostages held in the US embassy in the Iranian capital of Tehran. The hostage crisis, which lasted for 444 days from 4 November 1979 to 20 January 1981, was viewed by many at the time as the final chapter in America's catalogue of post-World War Two political and military blunders, a litany of miscalculations and incompetence that included such low points as the 1961 Bay of Pigs invasion in Cuba and the 1968 Tet Offensive in Vietnam. The hostage crisis is thought to have led directly to the defeat of Jimmy Carter in the 1980 presidential election and the subsequent ushering in of the Reagan era. It would have been a prominent touchstone of national disgrace in the US at the time *The Thing* was being made. A film about a group of ill-equipped Americans trapped in an inhospitable part of the world and unable to call for help released at a time when voters wanted to believe that under Reagan it was 'morning again in America' was always likely to struggle commercially.

8.   The masking of the men, apart from helping to build mystery, was also a production expediency. Carpenter made frequent use of stand-ins for the main actors in scenes so

it helped to be able to disguise them in this way. Wilfred Brimley was never actually in attendance during the location filming in British Columbia; the brief scene of him being taken drugged up to the toolshed features a padded out double.

9.   Keen viewers of The Shining will notice that when Wendy and Danny make their night time escape from the Overlook pursued by the axe-wielding Jack there are no clouds of condensing breath visible, which rather gives the game away that the scene was shot on a room temperature sound stage. By comparison many scenes in The Thing were filmed on refrigerated sets which caused the actors' breath to be visible, a technique that Carpenter's film shares with William Friedkin's The Exorcist which also employed on-set refrigeration to established a visible coldness for its exorcism scenes.

10. Compared to his fairly extensive use of a Panaglide camera in the making of Halloween, Carpenter actually used it sparingly on The Thing. Most of the smooth passages through spaces were actually achieved with regular dolly shots. No more than around half a dozen shots in the final film (or, put another way, about two to three days of camera hire) are clearly Panaglide-originated. Then, as now, Panaglide/Steadicam hire is expensive; back in the days of The Thing there were very few of these cameras available to anyone. Certainly lengthy location use of the equipment was beyond most films' budgets, so it's no surprise that none of the exterior British Columbia footage contains any Panaglide shots.

11. Kubrick's favoured 1.33:1 aspect ratio meant that upon The Shining's release on home video practically none of the picture was lost when viewed on most 1980s TV sets. In fact viewers saw more of it on TV compared to the slightly masked 1.85:1 theatrical ratio which cropped the top and bottom of the picture. All fine until the advent of the widescreen TV. Now everybody gets frustrated when their Shining Blu-ray disc plays with black bars to the left and right of the picture on their flat liquid-crystal display monitor. The Thing by comparison has experienced this issue in reverse. The earliest commercial videotape releases were presented courtesy of moderately shoddy pan and scan, meaning that a lot of Carpenter's claustrophobic edge-of-picture compositions were compromised. In these more informed times of properly letterboxed editions we can all now appreciate every bit of The Thing's sweaty paranoia.

12. Much has been made of just how (appropriately) imitative Morricone's score is of the typical Carpenter score style. The director revealed how it came about in Gilles Boulenger's 2003 book John Carpenter: The Prince of Darkness:

     [Morricone] had written several pieces for The Thing, and I told him that he was using too many notes for the title track and that he should simplify it. He did simplify it, and the title track that you hear is his. He did all the orchestrations and recorded for me 20 minutes of music I could use wherever I wished but without seeing any footage. I cut his music into the film and realised that there were places, mostly scenes of tension, in which his music would not work. Since we needed something, I secretly ran off and recorded in a couple of days a few pieces to use. My pieces were very simple electronic pieces – it was almost tones. It was not really music at all but just background sounds, something today you might even consider as sound effects. I used these pieces as unifying moments because structurally we had to redo *The Thing* at one point in the centre. I put them in there to glue together the film, but in no way was I trying to compete with Ennio's score. The score is his. (Carpenter, 2003:144)

13. Fans of *The Exorcist* might like to know that Humbaba was the brother of Pazuzu the wind demon, co-possessor of poor Regan MacNeil in the book and film. Pazuzu shared Humbaba's physical form hybridity, being part-man, part-lion, part-dog, with the talons and wings of an eagle, a scorpion's tail and a serpentine penis.

14. The alternative ending that featured in the censorious U.S. cable TV cut of the film ironically made the final resolution even more bleak than Carpenter's preferred finale. Inserted after the usual closing shot of the burning camp was a daylight shot of mountains, smoke and a dog running away from the scene, which rather confirms that the men's attempts to halt the spread of the organism has failed.

BIBLIOGRAPHY

Becker, Jacques, Rivette, Jacques and Truffaut François (1956) 'Howard Hawks' [interview] *Cahiers du Cinema* No.56, 4-17. Reprinted in English translation in Sarris, Andrew (ed.) (1967) *Interviews with Film Directors* 187-196. New York: Avon Books

Billson, Anne (1997) *The Thing (BFI Film Classics)*. London: BFI Publishing

Billson, Anne (2012) 'The Thing: Figures in the frame'. *Multiglom*, weblog post, 19 October 2012, accessed 18 November 2012

Boulenger, Gilles (2003) *John Carpenter: The Prince of Darkness*. Los Angeles: Silman-James Press

Brophy, Philip (1986) *Horrality - The Textuality of Contemporary Horror Films*. Screen 27 (1), 2-13

Campbell, John W; Nolan, William F (2009) *Who Goes There? The Novella That Formed The Basis Of "The Thing"*. Rocket Ride Books

Ciment, Michel and Niogret, Hubert (1992) *Interview at Cannes* in Peary, Gerald (ed.) (1998) *Quentin Tarantino: Interviews*. Oxford: Roundhouse Publishing Ltd

Cohen, Stuart (2012) 'The Cast and Crew Screening'. *The Original Fan*, weblog post, 11 June 2012, accessed 11 December 2012

Cohen, Stuart (2012) 'The Sound'. *The Original Fan*, weblog post, 29 April 2012, accessed 13 December 2012

Creed, Barbara (1993) *The Monstrous-Feminine: Film, Feminism, Psychoanalysis*. New York: Routledge

Elkins, James (1999) *Pictures of the body: pain and metamorphosis*. Stanford: Stanford University Press

Gianetti, Louis (2010) *Understanding Movies*, 12th ed. Upper Saddle River NJ: Pearson

Girard, Gaïd (1996) *Au-dessus du labyrinthe : à propos d'un extrait de* The Shining *(1980) de Stanley Kubrick.* La Licorne 36, 181-192

Grant, Michael *The Thing* in Cook, Pam and Bernink, Mieke (1999) *The Cinema Book,* 2nd edn. London: BFI Publishing

Hartl, John (1992) Is There An End In Sight For The Happy-Ending Trend? *The Seattle Times* 27 November 1992

Hickenlooper, George (1991) 'John Carpenter: The Banality of Evil' in *Reel Conversations: Candid Interviews With Film's Foremost Directors and Critics*: 329-343. New York: Citadel

Hogan, David J, Mayo, Michael and Jones, Alan (1982) *I Don't Know What It Is But It's Weird and Pissed Off.* Cinefantastique 13 (2/3): 48-75

Johnson, William (1972) *Focus on the Science Fiction Film* Upper Saddle River NJ: Prentice Hall

Kristeva, Julia (1982) *Powers of Horror: an Essay on Abjection.* New York: Columbia University Press

Lovecraft, H.P. (1936) 'At the Mountains of Madness' in *Astounding Stories* 16 (6): 8-32, 17 (1): 125-164, and 17 (2): 132-164

McKee, Robert (1998) Seminar for the Editors Guild at the Directors Guild of America, 6 May 1998. http://www.editorsguild.com/newsletter/RealAudio/audioindex.html; Audio Extract accessed 16 October 2012

Metz, Christian (1986) *The Imaginary Signifier: Psychoanalysis and the Cinema* Chichester: Wiley

Montag, Christian; Buckholtz, Joshua W; Hartmann, Peter; Merz, Michael; Burk, Christian; Hennig, Juergen; Reuter, Martin (2008) *COMT genetic variation affects fear processing: Psychophysiological evidence.* Behavioral Neuroscience 122 (4), 901-909

Gaines, William, M. (1954) Quote from: Senate Subcommittee on Juvenile Delinquency 'Testimony of William M. Gaines, publisher, Entertaining Comics Group, New York, NY.'

(Date: 21 April 1954) Text from: *TheComicBooks.com* http://www.thecomicbooks.com/gaines.html accessed 15 January 2013

Verniere, James (1982) John Carpenter: Doing His Own 'Thing' [interview]. Rod Serling's *The Twilight Zone Magazine* 2:8, 24-31

Welles, Orson (1958) 'Ribbon of Dreams' in Whitebait, William (ed.) *International Film Annual* No.2. New York: Doubleday

Wheatley, Ben (2013) 'Ben Wheatley's Top 10 Horrific Films' *Film4 Top Lists* http://www.film4.com/special-features/top-lists/ben-wheatley-top-10-horrific-films accessed 27 January 2013

White, Eric (1993) *The Erotics of Becoming: XENOGENESIS and The Thing.* Science Fiction Studies 20 (3) 394-408

DEVIL'S ADVOCATES

"Auteur Publishing's new Devil's Advocates critiques on individual titles offer bracingly fresh perspectives from passionate writers. The series will perfectly complement the BFI archive volumes." Christopher Fowler, Independent on Sunday

LET THE RIGHT ONE IN — ANNE BILLSON

"Anne Billson offers an accessible, lively but thoughtful take on the '80s-set Swedish vampire belter... a fun, stimulating exploration of a modern masterpiece." Empire

WITCHFINDER GENERAL — IAN COOPER

"I enjoyed it very much; it sets out all the various influences, both before and after the film, and indeed the essence of the film itself, very well indeed." Jonathan Rigby, author of English Gothic

SAW — BENJAMIN POOLE

"This is a great addition to a series of books that are starting to become compulsory for horror fans. It will also help you to appreciate just what an original and amazing experience the original SAW truly was." The Dark Side

THE TEXAS CHAIN SAW MASSACRE — JAMES ROSE

"[James Rose] find[s] new and unusual perspectives with which to address [the] censor-baiting material. Unsurprisingly, the effect... is to send the reader back to the films... watch the films, read these Devil's Advocate analyses of them." Crime Time

Printed and bound by CPI Group (UK) Ltd, Croydon, CR0 4YY

27/03/2025

14649114-0001